W9-DDC-239

A DEATH FEAST
IN DIMLAHAMID

OTHER BOOKS BY TERRY GLAVIN

Nemiah: The Unconquered Country (1992)
A Ghost in the Water (1994)
Dead Reckoning: Confronting The Crisis in Pacific Fisheries (1996)
This Ragged Place (1996)

WITH CHARLES LILLARD

A Voice Great Within Us (1998)

A DEATH FEAST IN DIMLAHAMID

Terry Glavin

NEW STAR BOOKS

VANCOUVER

1998

In memoriam
DAVE BOSTOCK
1949-1990

Copyright 1990, 1998 Terry Glavin

All rights reserved. No part of this work may be reproduced or used in any form or by any means — graphic, electronic, or mechanical — without the prior written permission of the publisher. Any request for photocopying or other reprographic copying must be sent in writing to the Canadian Copyright Licensing Agency (CANCOPY), 6 Adelaide Street East, Suite 900, Toronto, Ontario, M5C 1H6.

New Star Books Ltd.
2504 York Avenue
Vancouver, B.C.
V6K 1E3

Map by Vic Bonderoff
Photograph on page 219 by Steve Bosch
Printed and bound in Canada by Webcom Ltd.
1 2 3 4 5   02 01 00 99 98

Publication of the book is made possible by grants from the Canada Council, the British Columbia Arts Council, and the Department of Canadian Heritage Book Publishing Industry Development Program.

THE CANADA COUNCIL | LE CONSEIL DES ARTS
FOR THE ARTS | DU CANADA
SINCE 1957 | DEPUIS 1957

Canadian Cataloguing in Publication Data

Glavin, Terry, 1955-
  A death feast in Dimlahamid

  Includes bibliographical references.
  ISBN 0-921586-64-7

  1. Kitksan Indians — Land tenure. 2. Wet'suwet'en Indians — Land tenure. 3. Kitksan Indians — Claims. 4. Wet'suwet'en Indians — Claims. 5. Kitksan Indians — Social life and customs. 6. Wet'suwet'en Indians — Social life and customs. I. Title.
E99.K55G6 1998   346.71104'32'089972   C98-910416-8

CONTENTS

ACKNOWLEDGMENTS

My first gratitude is to the Gitksan and Wet'suwet'en hereditary chiefs. I am obliged by their endurance, dignity and good humour, and I offer this book to their ada'ox and kungax. Of the chiefs, I am especially thankful to the fireweeds' Wii Seeks for his guidance, his patience, his instruction and his good company. His example demonstrates something about how to be brave and do the right thing.

In and around the Gitksan and Wet'suwet'en homelands, there are many who fed me, looked after me and showed me the lay of the land. Among them are Gordon Sebastian, Shirley Meldrum, Soup Wilson, Josh McLean, Norman Moore, Ernie Muldoe, Bev and Ian Anderson, Herb George, Marvin George and Kenny Rabnett. On the way there, whenever I learned something about the depth of what I was up against, I learned because of people like Jacob Hope, Richard Bailey, Frank Malloway, Roger Adolph, Jimmy Scotchman, Faith Pierre, Keith Matthew, Wii Muugalsxw, Harry Chingee, Freddy Johnson, Ruby Dunstan, Sharon Russell, Linda Myers, Earl Claxton, Tom Sampson, Wendy Grant and Bevan Charlie. And there are those who were particularly generous in helping me learn. Among them are Mas Gak, Stuart Rush, Neil Sterritt, Saul Terry, Alan Haig-Brown, Cunliffe Barnett, Ed John and Stan Persky. And there are those who put up with me, encouraged me, offered suggestions, answered my questions and taught me questions to ask. They are Rolf Maurer, my brother Anthony, Steve Bosch, my oolichan fishing partner Ernie Crey, Loretta Williams, Teresa Marshall, Don Monet, and Vicky Russell of the chiefs' library in Hazelton.

I would also like to thank the editors of the *Georgia Straight*, my friends Rick Bailey and Diane Bailey, as well as Yvette Guigueno and our kids, Zoë, Eamonn and Conall.

A DEATH FEAST IN DIMLAHAMID

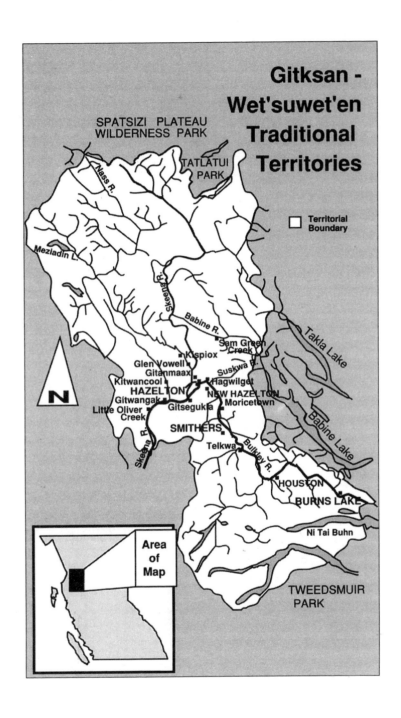

Gitksan - Wet'suwet'en Traditional Territories

SPATSIZI PLATEAU
WILDERNESS PARK

TATLATUI
PARK

Nass R.

Meziadin L.

Skeena R.

Babine R.

Takla Lake

Sam Green Creek

Kispiox

Glen Vowell

Gitanmaax

Suskwa R.

Kitwancool

Hagwilget

HAZELTON

NEW HAZELTON

Gitwangak

Moricetown

Little Oliver Creek

Gitsegukla

Babine Lake

Skeena R.

SMITHERS

Telkwa

Bulkley R.

HOUSTON

BURNS LAKE

Ni Tai Buhn

N

□ Territorial Boundary

Area of Map

TWEEDSMUIR PARK

ONE

DELGAMUUKW
VERSUS
THE QUEEN

It was early on the morning of September 7, 1987, at Morice-town, an old Wet'suwet'en village above a roaring canyon on the Bulkley River in British Columbia's vast northwest country. It was a cold, clear morning, and smoke from the village chimneys rose in thin blue lines into the sky. On a high promontory overlooking the river's twisting cataract, Adam Gagnon was busy at the controls of his back-hoe, levelling the ground for a garden behind his half-built new house. His wife, Georgian, was breaking clumps of earth with a rake behind him, and a raven was dancing in the light breeze above the hill, known in the old language as The Meeting Place.

Through the cab window Adam noticed something strange on the ground around the backhoe shovel. The dark, wet soil had turned a brilliant red. Gagnon held the controls stiff in his hands and leaned forward to get a closer look. He manoeuvered the bucket to one side, switched off the engine, climbed down out of the cab and walked around front. The ground was covered in ochre.

Throughout North America, red ochre has ceremonial associations just about everywhere it is found, and it often turns up when burial sites are disturbed. It was used obsessively by the Beothuks, those North Atlantic seagoing people known to Norse mariners as skraelings 800 years before French headhunters, Micmac refugees, English missionaries and disease caused their extinction. The Beothuks covered their bodies with it throughout their lives and buried their dead in graves of ochre. Even though seventeenth century accounts depict them with black, brown and sometimes yellow hair, it was the ochre that stuck in the European imagination, and the term "Red Indian" stuck along with it, long before the last Beothuk, a woman named Shanawdithit, died of tuberculosis in Newfoundland in 1829. Red ochre was a highly valued commodity right across North America, and it was mined and traded through the vast networks of commerce that linked pack trails with coastal trade routes. On the continent's northwest coast it was mixed with oils to paint pictographs and to colour masks, and it was applied in the decoration of heraldic and mortuary poles. Used as body paint, it provided protection against insects and frostbite. Even the mountain goats, those great and shaggy half-mythical creatures in the high country to the northwest of the Wet'suwet'en homelands, were known to roll in outcroppings of it.

Adam knelt on the ground and picked up handfuls of it, and pieces of a skull fell through his fingers. In another handful was an arrowhead, then a spearhead, then hidescrapers, drills, bits of quartz, jade and obsidian. Then a stone bowl and a carved bone mortar. What Adam Gagnon unearthed that day was the grave of an important man, an individual of rank, almost certainly a priest. He had been buried with a collection of sacramental paraphernalia about 800 years earlier. There were only pieces of him left: a collarbone, pieces of his jaw, pelvis and leg bones. All his teeth had been filed to a uniform evenness.

On any other day, such a discovery would not have been considered quite so remarkable. But this time, Adam said, it was like an omen, and news of the find spread quickly through the community. The Wet'suwet'en people, and their more populous neighbours and allies, the Gitksan, say they have lived in the sprawling forests within the Bulkley and Skeena watersheds for perhaps tens of thousands of years, much longer than the time contemporary scholars put humans on this continent, which is conservatively about 12,000 years. The Gitksan and Wet'suwet'en sagas contain accounts of an ancient city state, known to the Gitksan as Dimlahamid and to the Wet'suwet'en as Dizkle, that spread for miles along the two rivers in the vicinity of their confluence. According to local traditions, the metropolis had to be abandoned after a series of wars and ecological upheavals associated with the mistreatment of mountain goats and retribution prompted by people who mocked the sky. In its heyday, it was the civilization that provided the crucible for the many cultures that emerged on the northern Pacific slopes of North America, societies that anthropologists credit with the most sophisticated forms of material culture ever developed by "hunter-gatherer" societies anywhere on earth, and probably the most elaborate North American societies north of Mexico. Strangely, no trace of the great feast halls and avenues of Dimlahamid/Dizkle has yet been found.

While pilgrims of Dimlahamid and Dizkle travelled west, east, north and south, the Gitksan and Wet'suwet'en, traditional allies though distinct in language and culture, returned to the mountains and valleys in the surrounding countryside. The historical record of the Gitksan and the Wet'suwet'en confirms a loose confederacy of hereditary chiefs in a complex society comprising more than 120 major "houses" within nine matrilineal clans that trace their origins too far back in time to document with contemporary scientific methods. Some anthropologists who have closely studied Gitksan and Wet'suwet'en society maintain that the hereditary names of the ranked chiefs are among the oldest continually held titles of any society on earth, and archeologists have determined a history of occupation along the Skeena and Bulkley rivers spanning at least 6,000 years. After a century of European colonization and disease, about 10,000 Gitksan and Wet'suwet'en remain, and about half of them still live in or near the Gitksan reserve villages of Gitanmaax, Glen Vowell, Gitsegukla, Gitwangak, Kitwancool and Kispiox, the Gitksan-Wet'suwet'en village of Hagwilget, and the Wet'suwet'en villages of Moricetown and Ni Tai Buhn.

The scores of pre-European village sites, fortified towns, camp sites and fishing stations in the Gitksan and Wet'-suwet'en territories often turn up artifacts of great antiquity like the drills and hidescrapers in the ochre-covered grave Adam Gagnon came across that morning in his garden. In 1898, at Hagwilget, a few miles downriver from Gagnon's house at Moricetown, Chief Johnny Muldoe was digging a posthole for his house when he found a hollow, clay-lined pit, at a depth of four or five feet, capped by a large stone. Under the stone he found 35 intricately carved stone batons, some of which showed traces of ochre. They were cylindrical, some almost two feet in length. They were sculpted to depict fish and birds, and evidently they were not meant for use as weapons of war. By an odd coincidence, A. W. Vowell, B.C.'s superintendent of Indian Affairs, was in nearby Hazelton on a tour of inspection at the time, and he somehow obtained the batons from Chief Muldoe. The local Indian agent, R. E. Loring, reported to Vowell later on that he had been told an old story accounting for the stone batons in which a woman, one of the few survivors of a devastating attack on the nearby village of Gitanmaax, had buried the weapons and insignia of her people in a cache at about the site of Chief Muldoe's posthole. She was said to have died in a repeat attack, taking the location of the cache with her to the grave. The story is noticeably similar to an origin saga of the Gitksan fireweed clan that takes place thousands of years ago at the advent of the time of Dimlahamid. In this account the woman's daughter marries the son of the Chief of the Sky, and she returns to earth with four children and with the crests the fireweed clan carry among its possessions to this day — the sun, the rainbow and the stars — and a magic stone baton, an earthquake charm. It is pointed at the enemy village, causing it to turn over, killing the inhabitants in revenge. The baton was lost, and the sky people moved to Dimlahamid. As it turns out, all but three of the stone batons Chief Muldoe dis-covered that day in 1898 have also been lost.

There was nothing much in Adam Gagnon's ochre-covered garden that morning that would normally prompt much excitement in this country, but for the belief among Gitksan and Wet'suwet'en people that everything has its cause and its own meaning.

On that same September morning, while Adam was kneel-ing above the unearthed sepulchre in Moricetown, lawyers for the Gitksan and Wet'suwet'en were walking up the stone steps of the Robson Street courthouse, an Arthur Erickson edifice of glass and concrete more than 600 miles to the south. They were headed for courtroom 53 of the B.C. Supreme Court to begin the first day in Vancouver of a trial in which the Git-ksan and Wet'suwet'en were forced to open their graves to prove they existed, to a government that formally denied they existed. They set out to prove that the Gitksan and Wet'-suwet'en have a history, speak their own languages, and hold a system of laws, of government, and religious beliefs.

If the Indians were found to be right and the B.C. government wrong, it could potentially restore the aboriginal authority over 22,000 square miles of land the B.C. government claimed as its own. It was the most important land claims case to come before a court in Canadian history.

The trial — known formally as *Delgamuukw versus The Queen*, Delgamuukw being the first of the 54 chiefs named as plaintiffs in the action — had actually begun on the morning of May 11 in the Bulkley Valley town of Smithers. Back then the lawyers were talking about six months of trial time, but a few weeks into the trial it became evident that this was not going to be quite like any other trial in the history of challenges before the courts within the realm of Indian grievances commonly known as "land claims." Over the protests of the hereditary chiefs, the trial had been moved to Vancouver. It would be almost three years before all the evidence was in, the various parties would spend in excess of $20 million on research and legal fees, and even then it would not be over.

It didn't take B.C. Supreme Court Judge Allan McEachern long to realize that this trial was going to be very different from any he had dealt with during his 36 years as a lawyer and a judge. A hard-working, quick-witted, 61-year-old asthmatic, McEachern was also an eastside Vancouver boy, a brutal rugby player, a non-drinking, non-smoking Coca-Cola addict with little patience for anything that hinted of a courtroom spectacle or a theatrical display. But before him was a case that demanded an unprecedented departure from normal rules of evidence, one that presented him with an uncomfortable range of rulings. At one extreme, he could hand down a decision that could in the end dismantle most of the Province of British Columbia and return it to the Indians. On another extreme, he could destroy more than a century of hopes held by the native people of Canada's

Pacific slopes and perhaps change the course of history in a direction in which the indigenous peoples of Canada's far west would be left a mere shadow of a distant past.

Certainly there had been aboriginal rights cases before, throughout North and South America and throughout Britain's former colonies the world over, and McEachern had a well-travelled path of case law to follow. Various courts and legislatures had reluctantly grappled with the legal rights held by Indians ever since Charles V, the King of Spain, convened a junta of lawyers and theologians in 1550 at Valladolid in an effort to square conquest with justice in Spain's new "possessions" in Mexico and Peru. At Valladolid, the two leading antagonists were Juan Gines de Sepulveda, who held that some races were simply superior to others and some were destined to servitude, and Bartolomé de Las Casas, who argued that indigenous peoples of the newly discovered continent possessed inherent rights to sovereignty and freedom. Just how the participants concluded the debate is lost to history, and King Charles V entered a monastery soon afterwards. But in more than four centuries since Valladolid, Canadian law had still not quite settled either on the side of Sepulveda or in favour of Las Casas.

Throughout the 1970s and 1980s, in a growing number of cases before Canadian courts, judges were finding something that came as quite a surprise to most British Columbians: there was merit, after all, in the old Indian argument that Indian title to the land west of the Rockies — the greatest amount of which was "Crown" or public land — had not been clearly ceded to the Crown from the indigenous peoples who lived there. This might be Canada, but whether or not it was legitimately British Columbia was becoming increasingly unclear. Judges did not quite know where to turn, and neither did the forest companies, who were meeting stiff resistance from Indians as their loggers moved deeper into the hinterland with rapid-rate clearcutting technology and improved road networks. Neither did the fishing companies, who were finding their century-old monopoly on commercial fishing challenged in the courts by Indian fishermen who defied them to produce evidence that any Indians had ever surrendered rights to the coastal fisheries resources. Mining companies were roadblocked until they talked terms on Indian hiring quotas. Even the all-powerful railway companies were spur-lined with court injunctions by small groups of Indians who fished salmon with dipnets from precarious perches in the Fraser canyon.

Given the depth and breadth of the case before McEachern, the courts would have to come to that fork in the legal trail, to that place that already existed in the real world, and there would have to be some kind of decision, even though whatever McEachern decided could be challenged eventually by one interest or another to the Supreme Court of Canada, even to the United Nations, as had occurred in 1981 in the Lovelace case. That was the case in which Ottawa was backed into a corner by a UN human rights tribunal and forced to repeal a section of the Indian Act even though it had been upheld by the Supreme Court of Canada. The Act had denied Indian status to Indian women who married non-Indians, and it also denied status to their children.

The Gitksan and Wet'suwet'en were leading the indigenous nations on the Pacific slopes on this most crucial issue, the "land question." What the hereditary chiefs were seeking was a clear declaration from the courts that all their traditional lands were still unceded, that provincial law held no sway, that Gitksan and Wet'suwet'en house chiefs were the only legitimate authority in their territories. Before Canadians was the very real possibility that Dimlahamid was not a myth, that it was British Columbia that was the myth. It was a difficult notion for most British Columbians to comprehend. The uncertainty caused a state of affairs that demanded the attention of Canadian law.

In the United States, the American cavalry, backed by American law, had sorted out this kind of uncertainty during the preceding 150 years. American governments had embraced solutions of genocide, treaty-making and treaty-breaking. Sometimes the army just horse-traded peace for reservations within which the surviving indigenous nations could enjoy limited rights to sovereign government. In the American states bordering British Columbia, each of those solutions had been embraced with varying degrees of enthusiasm. Almost immediately after the Americans wrested control of the entire Pacific coast mainland south of the 49th parallel in 1846, a half-century of relatively healthy relations between the races came to an end with the Crown's withdrawal. Within a year, lawlessness prevailed. In 1855 and 1866, Indians in what is now Washington state were slaughtered indiscriminately. Northern Indians who frequented Puget Sound ports were warned that their presence would from then on constitute a capital offence, and white citizens at a meeting at Port Townsend resolved to shoot on sight any Northern Indians found in American waters.

One of the most ominous reports about the new American regime came in the summer of 1877 from across the sage hills south and east of the Okanagan territory. Chief Joseph and the Nez Percé, on a long march to escape confinement on an Idaho reservation that had been set aside for them, were headed north to what they hoped would be freedom in Canada. Their protracted rear-guard battles with American soldiers had left scores of Nez Percé dead, but their bravery inspired some young Okanagans and Shuswaps on the Canadian side of the border. At a conference that summer at the head of Okanagan Lake, the young men urged an armed common front to defend themselves against unwanted white settlement. Fortunately for the outgunned Canadian authorities, delegates to the conference opted for a non-violent approach. For the Nez Percé, a humiliating surrender led them not to the Idaho reservation, but to Fort Leavenworth, Kansas, where a hundred more of their number died of disease. The rest of them were shipped to a lifeless plot of open land in the short-lived "Indian Territory" established by the U.S. Congress in the midwest, where the survivors succumbed to malaria. The fate of the Nez Percé was shared by hundreds of thousands of indigenous people throughout the American west: the Cherokees on their Trail of Tears, the Santee Sioux in their prison camps on the Minnesota River, the Tule Lake Modocs in the deep crevices of their Lava Beds, the Kiowas at Palo Duro, the Cheyenne at Hat Creek Bluffs, and then on December 29, 1890, the final massacre of the 300 Ghost Dancers at Wounded Knee.

On the British and Canadian side of the line, a different official policy prevailed. It is enshrined in the Royal Proclamation of 1763, a constitutional document beyond the power of Parliament to rescind, a document that has never been repealed and remains part of the body of Canada's constitution. The Proclamation states that nations and tribes with whom the Crown is connected, that live under the Crown's protection, shall not be disturbed or molested or suffer their lands to be bought privately or granted to settlers without the Indians' consent through public treaty-making. Largely because of the principles enshrined in the Proclamation, several Indian nations sided with the Crown during the American Revolution of 1776. After the American victory, the Crown's allies from the Iroquois confederacy were made refugees and fled north to Canada. Among them were John Deserontyon, who settled with his Mohawks on the north side of Lake Ontario at the Bay of Quinte, and the great war chief Joseph Brant, who was accompanied by thousands of Mohawk, Tuscarora, Onondaga, Seneca, Oneida and Delaware who settled in villages along Ontario's Grand River. Then there was the great Shawnee chief and Canadian hero Tecumseh, who held the rank of brigadier-general among the Canadian forces during the War of 1812. Tecumseh's dream of a military front of Indian nations united against American expansion in the midwest died with him at the Battle of Moraviantown. In the War of 1812, Canadian sovereignty was successfully defended against the Americans, thanks in no small part to Tecumseh and the warriors he rallied behind him.

Still, despite the loyalty of the Crown's indigenous allies, the principle of Indian sovereignty and land cession by tribal consent was applied so crudely as to make something of a mockery of the Proclamation's intent. Prior to Confederation in 1867, there had been land exempted from the Proclamation all along the Saint Lawrence River and out to the Gaspé, colonial treaties in southern Ontario, and the Robson-Superior and Robson-Huron treaties of 1850. In the maritime provinces, the Indian title was all but ignored. After Confederation, John A. Macdonald and his successors pushed the Canadian dominion westward, and treaties were secured by land-hungry speculators and railway-minded federal officials along the way. They preyed upon Indian nations at times when they were reeling from the effects of epidemic diseases or the famines caused by the decline of the buffalo herds of the prairies. If there was any doubt where Ottawa would stand if its intentions in the west were challenged, the Red River rebellion and the Northwest rebellion and the dead in both conflicts made matters clear. Such treaties as were obtained were routinely ignored or were interpreted by Ottawa in a narrow fashion. The "Numbered Treaties" were concluded between 1871 and 1929 and in the process, most of the Canadian landmass was ceded by the Ojibwa, Assiniboine, Cree, Blackfoot and Sarcee for white settlement and industrial expansion. But the principles of 1763, however crudely, were more or less followed.

Then the treaty makers reached the Rocky Mountains. That's where everything changes.

On the Pacific slopes of the continent, even the "Indians" themselves bear little relation to anyone the colonizers encountered east of the continental divide. Most of them don't even look like "Indians." They are often stocky, full-bearded, and not unlike the Japanese or the coastal peoples of Kamchatka. The pioneer anthropologist Franz Boas, who almost singlehandedly introduced the complex societies of the Pacific coast to Euro-American academia, once remarked that it was not until he made his first journey eastward from the Pacific coast to the Rocky Mountains that he finally met his first "real Indian." The origins of the peoples of the Pacific slopes also challenge the contemporary scientific theories on migrations from Asia to North and South America, but science is slow in these matters. As recently as 1858, the now-venerable Smithsonian Institute refused to believe that Indians could have constructed the mound earthworks in Ohio, and until the turn of the century, mainstream Christians still held that indigenous peoples may well have descended from one of the lost tribes of Israel, and their presence in North America certainly did not go so far back as 6,000 years, since that was the time of Adam and Eve's fall from grace. Into the 1920s, human occupation of the so-called New World was held by the scientific community to reach back not more than 4,000 years, and the prevailing view is that "paleo-Indians" migrated across the Bering land bridge from Siberia about 15,000 years ago as the subcontinent of Beringia fell below Arctic seas, swollen from the melting ice age. Recent evidence suggests that if footprints could be found on the floor of the Bering Sea they may well be seen to go in both directions, and a more likely scenario for the origins of the peoples of the Pacific slopes would involve complex patterns of migrations around the North Pacific, continuing systems of trade, and trans-oceanic cultural diffusion. The most recent studies in dental morphology have opened a wide window to indigenous peoples' origins in northern Asia, but those same studies, conducted by the foremost researcher in the field, Christy Turner of Arizona State University, lead to a conclusion that the Pacific slopes were settled by people who were different from all other indigenous peoples in North America, and that they are neither Indians, Eskimoan or Aleutian.

At the time Europeans arrived in the New World, almost half the indigenous peoples who lived in what is now Canada lived in what is now British Columbia. Of the hundreds of languages spoken in what is now Canada, each fell into one of eleven broad linguistic groups — in the same way that Indo-European is a linguistic group — and seven of those eleven linguistic families occurred in what is now British Columbia. Along the coast and along the rivers that empty into the Pacific, the societies that had flourished for the millennia before Spanish and English explorers arrived in their ships provided a quality of life that in many ways exceeded that attained by the common people in the countries of Spain and England. Among those societies are the Gitksan and Wet'suwet'en, the Tsimshian, Tlingit, Nisga'a, Tahltan, Haida, Kwagewlth, Heiltsuk, Nuxalk, Nuu-Chah-Nulth, Coast Salish, Nlaka'pamux, Lillooet, Secwepemc, Chilcotin, Carrier, Okanagan and Kootenay. The rich natural resources of the Pacific slopes, particularly the salmon runs, were harvested in a manner that allowed the development of densely populated towns and villages throughout the coast and along the rivers well into the interior, with far-flung trading empires that reached deep into the hinterland. And unlike many other regions of North America, west of the Rockies the indigenous peoples exploited their trade relations with the European powers to great advantage. On the coast they remained in complete command of their territories for a century after the first arrival of Europeans, and over much of the landmass, for a lot longer than that.

By the time the colony of British Columbia entered Confederation as a province in 1871, only a handful of minor treaties had been negotiated west of the Rockies, and those were within the bounds of the former colony of Vancouver Island. The Royal Proclamation of 1763 was regarded by the leading officials of the new province with open contempt. Elsewhere in the west, Ottawa controlled public lands within the Crown's jurisdiction so treaty settlements and land cessions were easily expedited, but B.C. was already a self-governing colony when it entered Confederation, and Victoria held that the province was in control of public lands despite the absence of treaties that extinguished aboriginal title and despite the absence of a valid claim to possession by right of conquest. To call British Columbia's political leaders racist is to understate the case in the extreme. They clearly fell into the theoretical camp defended by Sepulveda at Valladolid. An early advocate of Confederation with the unlikely name of Amor de Cosmos, an editor of the Victoria *Colonist* who was to become the new province's second premier, stated in 1863 that white people could no more talk about the Indians' right to land "than we can prate of the natural right of a he-panther or a she-bear to the soil." He went on to write: "If they trespass on white settlers punish them severely. A few lessons would soon enable them to form a correct estimation of their own inferiority, and settle the Indian title, too." The chief architect of B.C.'s position on the Indian land question was Joseph

Trutch, chief colonial commissioner of lands and works, and later B.C.'s lieutenant-governor. One of the key players in the establishment of Canada's Pacific province and the shadowy engineer behind the Terms of Union with Canada in 1871, Trutch was perhaps the most powerful force in the white community from the late 1850s to the early 1870s. It is Trutch's legal defence against Indian claims of unceded title that the B.C. government used in 1987 for its legal defence against the Gitksan and Wet'suwet'en in *Delgamuukw versus The Queen*, and for its general policy on the unresolved land question. In an 1850 letter to his wife, Trutch refers to Indians as "the ugliest and laziest creatures I ever saw," and 21 years later his attitude hadn't changed. In an 1871 letter to the secretary of state for the provinces, Trutch writes: "I have not yet met with a single Indian of pure blood whom I consider to have attained even the most glimmering perception of the Christian creed," and he goes on to say that the Indians are incapable of grasping "any abstract idea."

In the years that followed B.C.'s entry into Confederation, however, it became apparent that B.C.'s Indians were capable of grasping abstract ideas with a much firmer grip than Trutch himself. It had become obvious to native leaders in the early 1870s that B.C. had entered the Canadian union under terms that contained a serious flaw. On paper, B.C. controlled public lands, and the "Indian title" was presumed to have been extinguished. Trutch and his colleagues could say what they liked, but the land was still Indian land, and the federal government discovered much to its chagrin that it had to agree with the Indian position, that there was a fundamental problem with its new province, this "spoilt child of Confederation." In 1874, Federal Justice Minister Telesphore Fournier pointed out that on the B.C. mainland, "no surrender of lands has ever been obtained from the Indian tribes inhabiting it, and that any reservations which have been made, have been arbitrary on the part of the government, and without assent of the Indians themselves." Canada had been duped, as the federal minister of the interior, David Laird, pointed out in a memorandum of the same year. Referring to Article 13 of the Terms of Union, which stated that Ottawa would assume trusteeship in the matter of Indian lands in B.C. and that "a policy as liberal as that hitherto pursued" by B.C. should be carried on in the new province by Ottawa, Laird writes: "When the framers of the terms of admission of British Columbia into the Union inserted this provision, requiring the Dominion Government to pursue a policy as liberal towards the Indians as that hitherto pursued by the British Columbia government, they could hardly have been aware of the marked contrast between the Indian policies which had, up to that time, prevailed in Canada and British Columbia respectively." The following year, in 1875, B.C.'s Land Act was disallowed because of the unresolved land question. In September 1876, Lord Dufferin, Canada's governor-general, also protested B.C.'s refusal to acknowledge aboriginal title and urged the province to come to terms with the problem.

The province refused to budge, and in the following years, despite the occasional lapse into honesty, such as Prime Minister Wilfrid Laurier's commitment in 1911 to see the matter addressed and resolved, the federal government embarked on a course of collaboration with provincial officials to bury indigenous resistance and constitutional law along with it. When push came to shove, Ottawa would stand by B.C. There was the national railroad Canada had promised the coast in return for Confederation, and it looked like it was going to be late by years and more costly than anyone imagined. Some British Columbians were growing restive and there was talk about pulling out of Confederation.

But B.C.'s Indians stood firm. They maintained a willing-
ness to enter into treaties, to permit non-native settlement
and co-operate in resource extraction and economic life with
non-native governments, a stance that has prevailed to this
day. Following the events of 1871, despite the fact that whites
remained a minority of the population for about twenty years
after B.C.'s union with Canada, no united military solution
to the land question was ever seriously considered by the
indigenous leadership.

After having enjoyed as first nations a comparatively stable
relationship with the Crown for almost a century along the
coast, Indian leaders opted to proceed on the land question,
often with the assistance of white supporters, by petition,
lobby and law. Joint federal-provincial reserve commissions
in 1876 and the McKenna-McBride commission of 1912-16
were met wherever they went with continued reference to
the unresolved land question and with a refusal to accept
arbitrary reserves in place of treaties and land cessions. The
Haida simply refused to name any areas they wanted set apart
for them in the Queen Charlotte Islands and the Gitksans
gave the reserve commissioners an equally cool reception at
Kitwancool, Gitanmaax, Kispiox and Glen Vowell. The
chiefs refused to co-operate in the naming of village sites or
burial grounds until the question of aboriginal title had been
addressed. There was an apparent disbelief among chiefs that
in the end they would get anything less than justice, a senti-
ment evident when a Gitksan chief asked provincial authorities in 1884: "How can it be right for the white man to act so
to us?" In 1906, a delegation of chiefs led by Joe Capilano
visited London to present their complaints to the English
chief, King Edward VII. They told him their land title had
not been extinguished, non-natives were taking up their
lands without authority, all appeals to Ottawa had been
rebuffed and they were denied the vote. Another delegation

representing twenty tribes returned to London with the same grievances in 1909, the year the Allied Tribes of British Columbia was formed. In 1910, non-natives began to rally to the first nations' cause. The "Friends of the Indians" organization was formed in Victoria to provide assistance and lobby provincial officials, and in Ottawa, the Rev. A. E. O'Meara organized the Moral and Social Reform Council of Canada to lobby federal officials. By 1913, the Nisga'a retained the London law firm of Fox and Preece to file a petition before the Privy Council, which was the highest court in Canadian law at the time. In their petition, the Nisga'a asked that their title to their traditional territories be recognized as demanded by the Royal Proclamation of 1763, but the Privy Council chose not to consider it because the petition hadn't been sponsored by the Canadian government. In 1919 the Allied Tribes began a major organizing drive in the southern interior and appointed James Teit, a Scottish translator, anthropologist and settler among the Nlaka'pamux as its special agent. The bolstered troops from the interior turned the Allied Tribes into the larger Alliance of Indian Tribes.

With delegations criss-crossing the province, the country and the Atlantic ocean, the campaign for legal resolution of the title question at the highest courts available was developing into a formidable effort, and an uneasy truce prevailed between natives and non-native settlers throughout the Pacific slopes. On Saint Patrick's Day, 1920, the governor-general's office in Ottawa replied that no action would be taken on B.C.'s land question and the decision was "final." Three years later, after Mackenzie King came to power, that decision was reversed, and Ottawa pledged to assist in a legal resolution of the question, but the pledge was never honoured. Discouraged, the Alliance of Tribes resigned itself to seek redress on the land question before a special Parliamentary committee in Ottawa, but B.C. Premier John

Oliver stated that he would have nothing to do with it, and the committee sat for three weeks before issuing a decision on April 14, 1927, that would mark defeat in the 56-year post-Confederation effort to resolve the land question in the legal system. The Dominion of Canada would not allow the matter to be settled at law by referring it to the Privy Council, and in an odd twist, the committee decided that in the absence of treaties west of the Rockies, Ottawa would provide annual payments in B.C. of $100,000 for the Indians' technical training, hospitals, and the promotion of agriculture and stock-raising, a fiscal anomaly known for decades to follow as the "B.C. Special."

To suppress further Indian agitation and to silence the likes of O'Meara and Teit, the committee decision was reinforced with an amendment to the Indian Act that secured jail terms for any Indians who raised money to organize around the land question or to advance any land claim. Jail terms were also included for any lawyer who was formally retained to advance a land claim. The law remained in effect until 1951, and served as the flagship in a fleet of repressive laws that Ottawa and Victoria busied themselves with in the years following Ottawa's discovery that Canada's Pacific province was not in lawful possession of the land it claimed.

Indians were expressly denied the provincial vote in B.C. until 1949 and were denied municipal voting rights until 1948 (Indians across Canada were denied the federal vote until 1961). While the arbitrary reserves in B.C. were being established according to a general formula of ten acres per head of household, non-natives were permitted to pre-empt up to 320 acres of Indian land per person, but natives were explicitly prohibited from pre-empting land as a white person could without the written permission of the lieutenant-governor.

The very heart of Indian society on Canada's west coast, the feast system, was attacked in law from 1884 onwards. The feast, generally known as the potlatch, is the seat of government, the land titles office, the court, the theatre, the art gallery and the library of west coast cultures. From 1880 to 1951, attendance at a potlatch was punishable by jail terms of two to six months. White people who kept a lookout for the Indian agent while a feast was in progress were similarly subject to imprisonment. Until 1951, the law was broad enough to impose one-month jail terms for Indians who attended fiddle dances, agricultural exhibitions, rodeos, performances, pageants or shows without the explicit permission of the superintendent-general in Ottawa or an Indian agent (some Assiniboine Indians found themselves in the position of having to write Ottawa for permission to hold a Thanksgiving Day parade).

By 1920 the Indian Act was amended to require the compulsory attendance of Indian children in schools. In B.C., residential schools had already been constructed from the far northern bush country to the Gulf of Georgia. The express purpose of the schools was to teach children that their parents' ways of life were savage, and "civilization" was their only hope. Successive generations of Indians were robbed of a family life and in many communities the majority were robbed of the most basic skills required in parenting. In 1920 the Indian department's deputy superintendent, Duncan Campbell Scott, made clear the purpose of the schools: "Our object is to continue until there is not a single Indian in Canada that has not been absorbed into the body politic, and there is no Indian question and no Indian department."

In 1889, as the fish canning industry began its boom on the west coast, the fishing companies found that the coast's indigenous peoples — many of whom had been engaged in "commercial" river fishing by sales to the Hudson's Bay Company for 50 years — were the only reliable fishermen available to them, and the native people's skills and intricate knowledge of the fisheries resource made them powerful partners in the coast's fisheries as well as valued suppliers to area markets. So the Fisheries Act provided that from 1889 forward, Indians could no longer sell fish or own fishing licences. If they wanted to catch fish for anything other than their own food — this is the origin of the so-called "food fishery" on Canada's west coast — they would have to use licences owned by the fishing companies and sell fish to those companies. White fishermen, of course, could apply for their own licences. The canneries were assured a captive labour market of Indian fishermen who were paid five cents a fish, and a growing population of semi-independent white fishermen who were paid ten cents a fish. It was not until 1923 that Indians were allowed to apply for fishing licences as a white man could. As for selling fish, most Indians were effectively prohibited from doing so under any circumstances by regulations that prohibited upriver commercial fishing. Most Indians lived along the rivers, and the sale of fish caught above the tide line was still prohibited in 1987 when Adam Gagnon stood on the ridge above Moricetown with pieces of a human skull in his hands the day *Delgamuukw versus The Queen* began in Vancouver.

Long before European contact on Canada's Pacific slopes, the indigenous population may have numbered in the hundreds of thousands. Disease had spread across the continent well in advance of white settlement, however, and by the 1830s the population may have fallen as low as 70,000. Native people remained the majority well through the 1880s, but by 1929, the native population had dropped, largely due to smallpox, measles, and influenza, to a low of about 22,000. In the 1980s, however, the population was well on its way to recovery with more than 60,000 on-reserve "status" Indians and perhaps an equal number that had either lost their status due to the discriminatory laws that were overturned in the

Lovelace case or were simply living off-reserve. Still, when *Delgamuukw versus The Queen* began in 1987, the Indian death rate was 9.5 per 1,000 compared to 6.1 per 1,000 in the general population. Infant mortality in native communities was more than twice the rate among non-natives. The average life expectancy among native Indians was ten years fewer than the average Canadian's 75 years. In 1980, unemployment rates among native communities in Canada were three times higher than the national average, and the 1980 average annual income for a native person was $7,000 compared to the Canadian average of $13,000. Indians were about three times as likely to commit suicide as other Canadians and three times as likely to die violent deaths. More than half the country's Indians lived in substandard housing, with one-third of the houses on federal Indian reserves lacking toilets and almost as many lacking running water. Pediatricians were warning that alcoholism in Indian communities was causing a devastation of Indian children "worse than smallpox," and tuberculosis was on the rise despite its virtual disappearance from the non-native population.

Among British Columbians, who numbered about three million by the time *Delgamuukw versus The Queen* was filed in court, life simply went on. The vast majority of British Columbians lived in the Lower Mainland, where the Indian was the artist who carved those lovely totem poles in Stanley Park, or the hollow-eyed drunk who begged change at the corner of Hastings and Carrall in Vancouver's downtown eastside. To some British Columbians, the "real" Indians wore feathered headdresses and rode horses and shook hands with the Mounties and went away a long time ago and that was about that.

Then, in 1973, the long-suffering Nisga'a came close to winning the argument they had attempted to put before the

Privy Council in London so many years earlier. The Supreme Court of Canada finally considered their case, and of the seven judges, six agreed that the Nisga'a had a rightful claim of aboriginal title to their traditional lands, comprising about 4,000 square miles of the Nass River watershed to the north of the Gitksan and Wet'suwet'en territories. Three judges ruled that the title was valid and could still be asserted, but the other three ruled that the aboriginal title had been extinguished by the effect of colonial statute. The seventh judge, Louis-Phillippe Pigeon, offered no opinion on the question of title and handed the Nisga'a the same decision they had received from the Privy Council so many years earlier, that they needed the government's permission to come before the court and they hadn't got it.

It was enough to shake Ottawa out of its torpor, however, and the tie decision among the six judges on the question of whether aboriginal title still existed on the Pacific slopes set off a strange and slow chain reaction. Ottawa started talking about treaty making again and developed elaborate bureaucratic comprehensive claims processes. There was progress in the unceded areas of northern Quebec and the Northwest Territories. Judges started to rule in favour of Indians and against encroachments they opposed. With much pomp and splendour Canada's constitution was at last patriated from Great Britain, and it affirmed aboriginal and treaty rights, but it left the aboriginal rights concept an empty box that the courts were expected to fill on their own time. Through the 1980s there were nationally televised constitutional conferences with Indian leaders at the table. There were roadblocks, On-to-Ottawa caravans in the campaign to enshrine Indian rights to self-government in the constitution, and public debates about aboriginal rights.

There was also a planet that some scientists said was dying for want of an ozone layer. Forest companies were tearing through the last great stretches of wilderness in North America, taking volumes of wood out of the forest that even the B.C. government, the great friend of the forest companies, conceded were far above the volumes the forests could sustain. B.C.'s total wood harvest in 1970 was less than 60 million cubic metres. Less than twenty years later, fewer workers were employed in the forest industry but the annual cut had reached nearly 90 million cubic metres. Four major corporate groups controlled 86 per cent of the cut on the entire west coast. Fishermen waited at the mouths of northern rivers for ancient races of pink salmon that simply did not return. The day *Delgamuukw versus The Queen* began in Vancouver, more than two million sockeye and pink salmon were swimming in great circles at the mouth of the Fraser River, a few miles away from the courthouse, and they weren't supposed to be there. About 100,000 coho salmon were expected at the mouth of the Fraser three weeks earlier, but they hadn't shown up. That summer, in Barkley Sound off the west coast of Vancouver Island, fisheries officials closed the salmon fishery for want of salmon, and a week later 350,000 sockeye showed up that weren't supposed to be there. Biologists talked about planetary climatic patterns and changes in ocean temperature and fisheries scientists said they were seeing things nobody had ever seen in the 70 years officials had been keeping records on returning salmon. A drought that had threatened a return to the dustbowl of the 1930s on the prairies had reduced the snowcap in B.C.'s high country to its lowest point in generations. In the 175 years since Tecumseh died of a bullet in the chest fired by an American soldier, acid rain from American smelters and power plants had covered much of southern Ontario, and 14,000 Canadian lakes were dead. In the century since the Métis were defeated in the Northwest rebellion, 80 per cent of the great prairie grasslands had vanished along with the buffalo. Also gone were the Dawson caribou, the sea otter and the Atlantic grey whale. In the 120 years since B.C. entered Confederation, two-thirds of the west coast's old-growth temperate rainforest had been cut down. In the four centuries since Valladolid, the world's population had risen from 500 million to five billion. Cities around the world were choking on their own garbage, toxins and carcinogens saturated the food chain, and animal and plant species were disappearing at the rate of 100 each day.

Then out of the north came a self-described unconquered people claiming a history reaching back to an ancient civilization called Dimlahamid, or Dizkle, that they abandoned centuries before the time of Christ. They talked about cyclical time rather than linear time, and a continuum between animals, humans, the land and the spirits that for the Gitksan is codified as law in something called the ada'ox, and for the Wet'suwet'en, the kungax.

In their statement of claim, each of the 54 hereditary chiefs named as plaintiffs in *Delgamuukw versus The Queen* assert that from time immemorial they have lived in their territories, governed themselves under the authority of their own laws and have maintained their territories accordingly. Further, the chiefs asserted, their authority had not been superceded lawfully and their ownership of the land had never been extinguished lawfully. What the chiefs asked from the courts was a declaration that not only did they once own about 22,000 square miles of territory in the Skeena and Bulkley regions before the arrival of Europeans in North America, but they continued to own their territories, that they were still there, and were consequently expecting a clear decision that acknowledged their rights of ownership and jurisdiction, a decision that acknowledged their rights to govern the area, and a ruling that those rights superceded the rights of the Province of British Columbia. A full victory would mean that from then on, Canada would consist of ten provinces, two territories, and some sort of autonomous region in the northwest corner of British Columbia in the shape of a bat with outstretched wings, about the size of New Brunswick. A full victory would open the door for similar declarations governing most of the British Columbia landmass, which remained Crown land, unceded land, potentially reducing British Columbia's jurisdiction to virtually nothing. The implications were staggering — the restoration of the aboriginal authority over a vast chunk of the North American continent, larger than France, almost as large as Washington, California and Oregon combined.

The B.C. government responded in the voice of Joseph Trutch. In their statement of defence, government lawyers denied that the Gitksan people exist. They denied that the Wet'suwet'en people exist. The B.C. attorney-general denied that the chiefs named as plaintiffs were chiefs at all, and echoing a 1919 argument used by British lawyers before the Privy Council against the Matabeles of Southern Nigeria, the attorney-general denied that the plaintiffs were even descendants of chiefs. B.C. specifically denied that the plaintiffs represented who they said they represented, it denied that the Gitksan were a people with a common language, law, culture or economy, and it denied the existence of a Wet'suwet'en people with a common language, law, culture or economy. The attorney-general also denied that the plaintiffs ever owned or governed the territories they claimed. For good measure the B.C. government enjoined the federal government as a co-defendant. In keeping with its historical choice that if it had to choose, it would side with B.C. over the Indians, Ottawa sent in its own lawyers to fight with all its resources on B.C.'s side.

In May of 1987 McEachern, the senior justice of the B.C. Supreme Court, sat behind the bench in the Alfred Avenue courthouse in Smithers, that sawmill, railroad and ski town with a Bavarian-theme main street halfway between Prince George and Prince Rupert, with the last trial of his career in front of him. The courtroom was packed with Indians. They were chiefs, nobles and commoners, old men, young women, old women, young men, children and infants. The hallway outside was packed with Indians. Across the street, a building was packed with Indians disappointed with McEachern's decision against allowing them to watch the proceedings via closed circuit television. The Smithers townsfolk milled around and wondered what the blazes was going on.

Before the judge, Alfred Joseph, a man who described himself as a Wet'suwet'en chief and identified himself as Gisday Wa, informed the court politely that although some people might think this is Smithers, it's actually the house territory of a chief by the name of Gyolugyet, of Kyas Yax, which is also known as the House of Woos. The next man to identify himself was Kenny Muldoe, who inherited the name Delgamuukw and all its duties from Albert Tait, the original plaintiff who died before the trial began. Delgamuukw told the judge the case had nothing much to do with Western notions about aboriginal rights, that it was really about territory and authority. Delgamuukw and Gisday Wa took turns explaining the circumstances to McEachern. Delgamuukw informed the court that the Gitksan and Wet'suwet'en chiefs had observed the European settlers in their territories for a century and that the chiefs were prepared to suggest that the newcomers might want to stay on in their towns and villages, but beyond the farm fences, a different law prevailed. "The Europeans did not want to know our histories," said Delgamuukw. "This ignorance and disrespect continues."

THE OFFICE OF GITKSAN
AND WET'SUWET'EN CHIEFS

NOTICE

GITKSAN AND WET'SUWET'EN TERRITORIES

THIS IS TO ADVISE YOU THAT YOU STOP
ALL UNAUTHORIZED ACTIVITIES WITHIN
THE FOLLOWING HOUSE TERRITORIES

LUDKUDZII WUS, XSIMWITS'IIN, DJOGASLEE,
AXTIIZEEX, GYETM GULDOO, YAGOSIP,
GOOHLAHT, CASPIT, SMOGELGEM AND WOOS

TRESPASSERS WILL BE DEALT WITH
ACCORDING TO GITKSAN LAW

BY ORDER OF

CHIEF *Lester Moore*
per *Ben MacKenzie*
LUDKUDZII WUS

CHIEF *Joyce Turner*
YAGOSIP

CHIEF *Lester Moore*
XSIMWITS'IIN

CHIEF *Mrs. Lucy Namox*
GOOHLAHT

CHIEF *Walter Wilson Sr.*
DJOGASLEE

CHIEF *Stanley Morris*
CASPIT

CHIEF *Bruce Johnson*
AXTIIZEEX

CHIEF *Leonard George*
SMOGELGEM

CHIEF *Martha Ridsdale*
per *Sylvester Green*
GYETM GULDOO

CHIEF *Roy Morris*
WOOS

DATE Sept. 27 / 89

THE WAR
ON THE LAND

It had gone on long enough. The war might well have to be won at law, but it was also quite clearly a war that would have to be fought on the land.

By the night of October 13, 1989, to a group of Gitksan and Wet'suwet'en chiefs sitting around a table at Gitanmaax Hall, it was also clear that if they were going to effectively enforce their September 27 order against unauthorized activities in the Suskwa region, the roadblock camp they had set up two weeks earlier on the Suskwa Main road, deep in the bush country north of Gitanmaax, would have to be moved further south, closer to Highway 16. A move south would protect a bigger chunk of countryside by blocking access to sideroads, and it would better protect the people maintaining the camp. The immediate aim of the Suskwa roadblock was to stop the logging companies from taking any more timber out of an area covering several hundred square miles and roughly bounded by the Skeena River to the west, the Babine River to the north, the Bulkley River to the south and the broad, fertile Bulkley Valley bottomlands to the east. But the Suskwa blockade also had its longer-term strategic value. The only road into the area was the Suskwa Main, and it was already cleared a few dozen miles in, as far as Gail Creek. A roadblock would prevent roadbuilding any further north, blocking access to the vast forests on the far side of the Babine River, an untouched wilderness that had figured in the long-range plans of more than a half-dozen forest companies from Hazelton to Prince George. It was a wilderness that the Gitksans had defended in a series of rear-guard roadblocks right up to the banks of the Babine River only a few months earlier.

Around the map-covered table at Gitanmaax Hall sat several of the Gitksan and Wet'suwet'en chiefs who had signed the September 27 order. They were joined by a small group of friends and relatives.

"Here's a good spot," said Gordon Sebastian. He's 39, a frog clan Gitksan, Hagwilget lawyer, board member for the Kitimat-Stikine Regional District and a key player in the Gitksan leadership. "The public can go through with their little cars but the logging trucks can't get through. It's a problem where it is now, you know? They can't see the camp. They're scared of Indians. White people are scared of Indians."

Sgenna, Sebastian's uncle, ran his right hand over the map, squinted through his glasses and ran his left hand through his crewcut. Sgenna is Delbert Turner, truck-logger and a member of the frog clan house of Ludkudzii Wus, one of the Suskwa chiefs. He has a big stake in the roadblock. His wife is Yagosip, another Suskwa chief, from the wolf clan. She sat beside Delbert, and looked equally concerned. Delbert shook his head. He wasn't impressed with Sebastian's pick of a new site on the road. The camp isn't secure where it is, he said, and any new site won't be secure unless it's well attended. "If twenty loggers get drunk in New Town one night, there would be nothing we could do."

It took them a while to make up their minds, but when they did, the decision was by consensus, as decisions usually are when the Gitksan and Wet'suwet'en are considering such matters. They would dismantle the roadblock camp, establish a new blockade and build a new camp in the bush nearby, on a wooded ridge above the Bulkley River, only a couple of miles in from Highway 16.

Wii Seeks was quiet throughout the discussions. Wii Seeks is 41-year-old Ralph Michell, also known as Tiger, a nickname he picked up as a result of his teenage reputation for never avoiding a fight in Gitanmaax, the hilltop reserve village overlooking the town of Hazelton. The nickname stuck during his days working in the sawmills, where he was the scrappy vice-president of the local union. Wii Seeks, a fireweed chief, was raised by Elsie Morrison, the high-ranking chief Waigyet of the same clan, and by David Gun-an-noot, son of Simon Gun-an-noot, the famous Gitksan outlaw who was charged with murdering a white man and a "half-breed" in 1906, but evaded provincial police and American Pinkertons in the remote northern reaches of Gitksan country for thirteen years until he turned himself in, stood trial, and was acquitted in a Vancouver courtroom on both counts in 1919. Wii Seeks had served as the tribal council's treasurer, president of the local legal services society and interpreter for the lawyers in *Delgamuukw versus The Queen*. For years, he had passionately advocated the kind of action the Suskwa chiefs were taking, and whenever the Gitksans stood up against the law, Wii Seeks was sure to be there. He was usually vocal at meetings such as this, but Waigyet, his grandmother, had died only days earlier, and Wii Seeks hadn't been saying much. After the talking was over, he made no speeches. He just said: "What you're doing here is good. I'm proud of you."

Wii Seeks had found much cause for pride in the late

1980s, when the hereditary chiefs embarked on a sort of non-violent guerrilla war, in tandem with the land claims trial, to defend their territories against increased logging activity.

If there was a Gitksan general in this war it was Mas Gak, with Wii Seeks as his chief lieutenant, and both had emerged among the principal voices of the Gitksan and Wet'suwet'en confederacy by the late 1980s. Mas Gak is a sophisticated, well-travelled and well-educated political strategist otherwise known as Don Ryan. He had been taking a higher profile in the community throughout the 1980s, and in 1987 he assumed the presidency of the Gitksan-Wet'suwet'en Tribal Council from Neil Sterritt, who had pioneered much of the early work on the land claims case. Sterritt went on to work for the Assembly of First Nations in Ottawa and Mas Gak, a fireweed and 41-year-old former social worker, began to disassemble the federally sanctioned structures of tribal council and band council in favour of more direct rule by the traditional authority of hereditary chiefs.

Mas Gak's strategy, supported by the chiefs and implemented by Wii Seeks, was that the chiefs should mean what they say, defend their territories and surrender nothing. While Attorney-General Brian Smith was saying that to negotiate peacefully with Indians was to go "the Neville Chamberlain route," Mas Gak was telling B.C.'s tribal leaders to be "prepared for war ... to confront the military apparatus of the country" to defend their territories. If that meant arresting police officers, do it, he said. If that meant shooting at helicopters with flares, do it, he said. In Gitksan country, it meant Radio Free Gitanmaax, a "pirate" radio station that operated without the benefit of a federal licence ("Our authority includes the airwaves," said Mas Gak), and it meant elaborate "illegal" bingo operations that drew players from as far away as Saskatchewan and offered $40,000 prizes and provided revenues to build schools on the reserves ("Historically, we have been known for our propensity to gamble. Bingo is an aboriginal right," said Wii Seeks).

But mostly, it meant logging road blockades.

It was becoming clear to most tribal leaders in British Columbia that even if they did get justice on the land question in the courts, there might be little left of the land's natural wealth when that day came. There seemed little sense in waiting for Ottawa's comprehensive claims process to unfold, or for a victory in *Delgamuukw versus The Queen*.

In Gitksan and Wet'suwet'en country, where the logging industry provided the greatest cash income for the minority of employable Indian adults with fulltime jobs, it was a challenge, a challenge Mas Gak described this way: "The roadblock is a test. You have husband against wife, brother against brother and father against son, the whole thing with Indian-white relations, and all that plays itself out. But it's the kind of discussion we have to have."

And if the roadblock was indeed a test of the authority the chiefs claimed in *Delgamuukw versus The Queen*, the Gitksans were clearly up to it. They had their own history of resistance to draw lessons from, all the way from the blockade of the Skeena River after the burning of Gitsegukla in 1872, through the battles with fisheries officers over the right to inland fisheries and the railway blockades at Gitwangak in 1985, and as the 1980s drew to a close, they could also look to the roadblocks erected by the Lubicons of Alberta, the Innu of Labrador, the McLeod Lake Sekanis, the Tahltans of Telegraph Creek and the Haidas of the Queen Charlotte Islands.

In some tribal territories, the law had been successfully used to put logging on hold while the question of aboriginal title remained unanswered. It was successfully used by the Nuu-Chah-Nulths at Meares Island in 1985, when the B.C. Appeals Court, the highest court in the province, granted an injunction against logging that spectacular little island off the west coast of Vancouver Island at the mouth of Tofino Harbour. The prevailing judgment, against the corporate giant MacMillan Bloedel, held that the Indians had for generations pressed the question of title, but "they have not been dealt with at all. Meanwhile, the logger continues his steady march and the Indians see themselves retreating into a smaller and smaller area. They, too, have drawn the line at Meares Island. The island has become a symbol to their claim to rights to the land." And the law was successfully used the following year at Deer Island, a small island between the mainland coast and Vancouver Island, in Kwagewlth territory. In that case, the Kwagewlths were able to use a "Douglas Treaty," one of that handful of colonial treaties on southern Vancouver Island, to prevail against Halcan Log Services in the Kwagewlths' campaign to maintain access to berry grounds, hunting areas and gravesites. On the Queen Charlotte Islands, the inequity of B.C.'s traditional position in the courts was used to secure the Haidas' control of the entire southern portion of their island homelands, but only after 72 Haidas were arrested at a Lyell Island logging road blockade. The federal and provincial governments tried to find an easy way out by compensating the forest companies and declaring the south Moresby region a park reserve, but the Haidas knew it for the victory it was — a restoration of their sovereignty in the area. At McLeod Lake, a Sekani village deep in B.C.'s northern bush and within the arctic drainage area covered by Treaty Eight, Chief Harry Chingee had grown tired from years of waiting for recognition of his band's treaty rights. He set up a logging road blockade in defiance of a B.C. Supreme Court injunction and in December 1988, he won from the courts an injunction preventing logging companies from clearcutting a vast area the Sekanis claimed as their treaty entitlement.

A formal attempt by the Gitksan and Wet'suwet'en to

restrain unwanted resource extraction in their tribal territories had failed in 1987, when the B.C. Supreme Court refused their request for an injunction against new logging areas or Crown land pre-emptions while *Delgamuukw versus The Queen* remained before the courts.

In the Gitksan and Wet'suwet'en territories, there were already 39 sawmills in operation by 1920. But they were small-scale outfits, and the forest industry developed slowly, at a pace the forests could sustain. Right up to the 1960s selective logging was practiced — only the best trees were cut, and traditional resource uses were not severely impacted. But with the advent of massive forest-clearcutting techniques, more lethal technologies and more productive mills with fewer workers, the scene was changing drastically, particularly following the recession of the late 1970s. Westar Timber, the major company in the region with a whole log chipper and two sawmills all within an hour's drive from the fabled lost city of Dimlahamid, employed 600 workers by 1989, consuming 1.5 million cubic metres of wood a year, almost ten times as much as it had consumed ten years earlier. At the Gitksans' northwestern frontiers, another million cubic metres of wood that had been virgin forest in the 1970s was being cut and shipped in whole logs every year out of the region, and in some cases, straight out of the country to Asia.

By the time the tribal leaders' attempts at an interim land freeze had failed before the courts in 1987, two thirds of the chiefs' traditional territories remained virgin forest. But where there was logging, independent foresters working for Silva Ecosystems Consultants Ltd. found the countryside turning to moonscape. An 82-page report cited wholesale overcutting and mile-wide clearcuts. Merchantable timber was left on the ground to rot in "high-grading" operations — cutting all the trees and taking only the best — and the soil in some house chiefs' territories was reverting to its condition at the close of the last ice age.

Throughout the Gitksan-Wet'suwet'en territories, while *Delgamuukw versus The Queen* proceeded slowly in B.C. Supreme Court, roadblocks were starting to turn up everywhere.

On February 11, 1988, at Little Oliver Creek, on the western frontier of Gitksan territory a few miles east of Terrace, the Gitksan frog clan chiefs of Gitwangak issued a notice to Skeena Cellulose and Tide Lake Logging that frog clan chief Luulak, Sandra Williams, would not permit any more logging on her house territory. Merchantable timber had been left to waste on the ground and some trees had been cut several yards from their base in what was obviously high-grading of good timber. About twenty Indians showed up at the site at 8:30 that February morning, warning the contractors to leave the area and informing them they had 24 hours to remove their equipment and if they did not heed the warning they would be treated as thieves. The RCMP was called in, but the three crew trucks backed off. "I don't want to have anything to do with this," Tide Lake's Frank Cutler said. "The Indians say they were never defeated and we never took their land. I don't know. I wasn't there." It was a clear and immediate victory. The next day, the police arrested Giila'wa, the 52-year-old eagle clan chief Peter Turley, on a charge of possession of stolen property. On Luulak's instructions, Giila'wa had removed a front-end loader that was left behind at the site. An angry Mas Gak said the case would be fought as far as needs be, pointing out that Giila'wa would be entitled to a trial by a jury of his peers — other Gitksan nobility — and further pointing out that Indians were effectively barred from jury duty in Canada until 1974, when jury selection was amended to permit selection from on-reserve voters lists. The case against Giila'wa was dropped.

Later that month, at about 3:30 a.m. on Monday the 29th of February, Mary Johnson, the 78-year-old Kispiox matriarch Antiigililbix, wrapped a traditional button blanket around her frail shoulders, walked through her old village, so famous for its totem poles, and stood at a bonfire in the middle of the logging road that dissects the reserve. Robert Jackson got into his pickup truck and with the help of a few of the younger men hauled a huge cedar log across the road, where on a normal day a fully loaded logging truck would pass every ten minutes in an annual convoy that took 500,000 cubic metres of wood, enough to build a city of 10,000 houses, out of the Kispiox Valley highlands. About twenty of the young men of the village were there already, and they stood around the blazing fire, stamped their feet on the frozen ground and tucked their cold hands deep into their pockets. Wii Seeks stood with them, beside Kispiox wolf clan chief Wii Muugalsxw, whose house territory entrusted to him under the Gitksan law of ascendancy was now in ruins, a barren ground several miles up the Kispiox Valley, scattered with cavernous pyramids of felled and discarded spruce trees. Wii Muugalsxw, who is the soft-spoken, 40-year-old Kispiox artist and carver Art Wilson, smiled nervously as the first logging truck showed up. Then the second, then the third, then the fourth, and it was all over the truckers' citizens band radio in minutes. RCMP Sgt. Fred Simpson arrived in his cruiser from Hazelton.

This wasn't Little Oliver Creek. This was one of the major conduits for timber supply in the entire northwest country. This time, things were going to be different, and Sgt. Simpson radioed in for backup.

Just before dawn, things turned nasty. There was confusion and shouting at first, and then trucker Jim Pierson turned and walked back to his truck. "This is bullshit," he said. "They've got enough already and yet they still have to screw us around." The other truckers followed Pierson, and by about 6 a.m. the truckers had set up their own roadblock on the far side of the Kispiox River bridge, within shouting distance of the village. If they couldn't get in, they weren't going to let the Indians out. Sgt. Simpson waited for word from the RCMP substation in Terrace, but there was still nothing definite. He talked the truckers into going home and waiting.

Then the sun came up. It was quiet around the fire, and the older women in the village brought tubs full of salmon chowder to the roadblock crew. Mary Johnson, old Antiigililbix, turned to the circle around the fire, and the men were quiet, and she sang them a song in the old language. And then she said, "I won't live much longer. I am standing here on behalf of myself, and my family, and my grandchildren and my great-grandchildren. They will be the ones to suffer all the trials and all the troubles." And then she sang some more.

Nothing moved, and the RCMP watched, wondering what to do. A few hours into the standoff, Sgenna, Delbert Turner, had agreed to move Robert Jackson's great cedar log to allow logging contractor Dave Webster to get his truck out from behind the barricade — Webster was among several truck loggers who were trapped inside the closed-off area when the blockade went up — on the understanding that Webster and the others would come to meet with the chiefs. But none of the truckers showed up at the Kispiox hall that night. Still, more than 60 truckers had been turned away from their rounds through the Kispiox Valley, so after three hours of debate, the chiefs decided to leave Robert Jackson's cedar log where it had been hauled away from the road. Never mind putting it back on the road just yet, said Sgenna, thinking a little further down the road. There was an old-time feast, and the decision was to fight another day.

The following morning, a chartered bus carrying 30 RCMP

officers in riot gear turned off Highway 16 into the parking lot of the Totem Cafe in the truckstop town of New Hazelton, a few miles from Kispiox. A second, empty bus rolled in behind the first, in case it was needed to transport Indians arrested at the roadblock. The RCMP force had been assembled from Mounties in Prince Rupert, Terrace and Smithers, and RCMP Supt. Ron Pettitt said it was a necessary "show of force" to see the blockade cleared. But the roadblock was already down.

Things were quiet again, for about two months.

On the morning of Thursday, May 5, on a road Westar Timber was pushing into rich forest lands on the northern frontiers of the Gitksan territories, Norman Larson of Al Larson Logging and six of his crewmen were on their way in to the head of the newly cleared road in the Salmon River area when they were stopped by seven Gitksans. There was no roadblock, just seven Indians who warned Larson's crew that they were trespassing on the house territory of Chief Gwoimt and would not be permitted to proceed further, and that they had until Saturday morning to get their equipment out of the area. Westar, the principal firm involved in the roadbuilding, had been invited months earlier to discuss its plans with the chiefs, but all the chiefs got were instructions to remove the traps from their traplines in the region.

The road was being built to provide a conduit for the timber Westar's mills needed in the Salmon River country, but its main function would be to provide a land connection to the vast forests north of the Babine River, in the territory of the old Gitksan villages of Kisgegas and Anlagasimdeex, a territory known to provincial forest ministry cartographers as the Sustut Block but known to the Gitksans as the house territories of their own chiefs, among them Wii Gaak (Neil Sterritt Sr.), Gitluudahl (Pete Muldoe), Wii Seeks (Ralph Michell) and Waigyet (Elsie Morrison, Ralph's grandmother). Standing with them as their neighbours were Miluulak, Tsabux, Wiiminosik, Luus, and Wiieelast. They were all fireweeds, frogs and wolves. Eight forest companies were in competitive bidding for a licence to log 400,000 cubic metres of Sustut timber every year for twenty years, but Westar was clearly the front-runner, with the rest of the companies on the far side of the region, in the Prince George area. The Gitksans said they needed the area, too, and so did the caribou and grizzly bear populations, which would be decimated by clearcutting. It was a spectacularly rich and roadless expanse of wilderness, several hundred square miles of untouched forests and mountains with the highest concentration of mountain goats west of the Rockies.

This was going to be it. It was one thing to highgrade the house territory of a chief west of Gitwangak. It was one thing to continue a regime of logging in the Kispiox Valley, where the provincial government had already committed the timber. But the chiefs had reached a decision on the government's plans to open up the northern territories with logging mains and sideroads: there would be no bridge across the Babine River.

For the other side, it was also time for a showdown. Keith Spencer, Westar's new manager of the company's northwest operations, said it was simply a police problem, and he would expect the police to act. There was no way the company could back off when a third of its anticipated timber supply in the coming years was at stake. As for all this carrying on about Gitksan house territories and unsurrendered Indian land, Spencer, only a few weeks on the job, said: "It's rubbish." Sgt. Simpson was called in again. He headed up the Salmon River road, said hello to everyone, and decided to "monitor" the situation this time, "in a peace-keeping capacity."

In tandem with *Delgamuukw versus The Queen*, the war would be fought on the land. Wii Seeks posed for an

American photographer's camera and said, "This is the last photo of Ralph Michell in peacetime." It was obviously going to be an interesting summer.

Then a war of injunctions began. The Gitksans applied for an injunction restraining the road-building while the main trial was still before McEachern. Westar applied for an injunction restraining the Gitksan from interfering in road-building. Wary of a quick defeat at law, the Gitksans made plans to pull back and establish a base camp deep in the roadless bush, near the old village of Kisgegas, on the south bank of the Babine River at Sam Green Creek. It was at that location that Westar intended to build its bridge, and directly on the far bank was the house territory of Wii Seeks. The Gitksans said if that was where they'd make their last stand, then they couldn't think of a nicer place, anyway. The situation may have been tense, but on September 15, 1988, as summer turned into fall, the chiefs established a bivouac on the Babine's south shore, at Sam Green Creek. While all the lawyers did the talking down in Vancouver, Sam Green Creek took on the atmosphere of a holiday camp. United Native Nations president Ron George, a Wet'suwet'en, spent his vacation at the camp, and the site was cheery despite the tension. There was the "Vancouver Five," a group of supporters from the Lower Mainland — Tom Sandborn, Penny Singh, Linda O'Hara, Jesse Frank and Carl Johnson — and another group of native supporters from Mount Currie spent much of their summer there as leaders like Sebastian, Wii Muugalsxw and Robert Jackson made the place as comfortable as they could. Yaya bounced out the long dirt road in his one-brake truck to bring out Antiigililbix, who turned up her nose at suggestions that the living was too rough for an elder such as herself, and Martin Nelson shot a sickly cougar that was making its last few slouching steps through the underbrush towards Herb

George. The people were comfortable enough, and their spirits were up for a showdown.

As the roadbuilders made their way steadily through the bush towards the Babine, autumn was in full colour and the mornings in camp were cold. Then Westar won a crucial interim injunction, on Tuesday, October 4 in B.C. Supreme Court. The injunction ordered the Gitksans to refrain from interfering with bridge surveyors, and the company's application for a permanent injunction was to go before the B.C. Supreme Court that Friday, October 7.

On Wednesday, October 5, a half-dozen Gitksans were at the camp when a convoy of process servers, RCMP officers and roadbuilders showed up at the edge of their camp. The visitors were warned to stay out of the camp, and Westar's woodlands manager, New Hazelton mayor Pete Weeber, complained that Wii Seeks had threatened him with violence if he came any closer. Wii Seeks said he wasn't concerned about their injunctions. "They're only going as far as they're at right now. The bottom line is there is going to be no bridge."

Lawyers for the Gitksan appeared in court on Friday to challenge the injunction's validity and applied for their own injunction against bridge construction. Justice Ray Paris took a look at the situation, which by this time had been complicated by the B.C. attorney-general's decision to intervene on the company's side. Judge Paris decided to take the weekend off to think things over.

It took three weeks for all the courtroom talk to subside, but when it did, the case was before Justice Alan Macdonell. The judge took umbrage at the Gitksans' behaviour, restrained them from any further disruption of the company's activities in the bush country south of the Babine River, and blasted the Gitksans for their "threats of violence and destruction." But he gave the Gitksans a victory. Westar and its bridge-builder, Formula Contractors, could build no bridge, at least while Delgamuukw and the rest of the chiefs were still suing the Queen.

The mood in the Gitksan camp was ecstatic. In Victoria, the attorney-general's office was strangely quiet. In Westar's corporate headquarters in Vancouver, the mood was grim, but grim with resolve, and with the provincial government's help, the case was taken to B.C.'s highest court, the B.C. Court of Appeal. In January 1989, the Gitksans took their roadblock to Vancouver and set up a campsite with a barrel-bonfire right on the courthouse steps, where they spent the night in tents and served soup and bannock on the sidewalk. By June, the decision was down. Two of the three judges agreed with the Gitksan and found against Westar and Victoria in a case the dissenting judge, Justice Charles Locke, predicted would "interrupt the established administrative and legal system" in British Columbia.

Mas Gak was jubilant. He referred to Locke's assessment of the situation and said it was the kind of interruption he thought would be just fine. Said Justice Locke: "In doing this, I cannot see why the interest of the entire province (in addition to that of Westar) in having a smooth-running system hallowed by law and by time does not outweigh the claim of the Gitksan." Mas Gak did not need to be told about law or about time.

Westar's Keith Spencer didn't like it any more than Locke did, but at least he had learned a lot about Gitksan law and about aboriginal title since he'd taken over as Westar's chief boss in the northwest fifteen months earlier. He said he wished everybody else understood just how serious this whole thing was getting. "This isn't just some little thing that has happened way up here. The whole province should be concerned about this. It's going to affect us all, whatever happens with all these land claims."

The following month, in July, after the frog, wolf and fire-weed clans had held up their end in the northern territories, the Gitksan eagle clan was taking a stand of its own on the Gitksans' western frontiers. Led by the eagle clan chief Giila'wa, who had been arrested for allegedly stealing a front-end loader during the Little Oliver Creek roadblock in the early spring of 1988, the Gitwangak eagles warned Skeena Cellulose that they didn't want any more unauthorized logging in the region. A blockade camp was set up in the bush directly in the path of a proposed logging road, and as the company's roadbuilders got closer, the company decided it had better talk. The chiefs and the company talked. A month later, the company agreed it would not attempt a confrontation, it would stay away from the courts, and it would develop with the chiefs a "mutually beneficial relationship in regards to sustainable development in the area."

After that summer had passed and the Suskwa chiefs, six of them Gitksan and four Wet'suwet'en, put their roadblock in place during those last days of September, there wasn't much but silence from the provincial government and there were no counter-roadblocks like the spectacle at Kispiox in 1988. There was also another Gitksan roadblock up north of Kitwancool, where Westar Timber pulled 25 loggers back from the Kitwancool River bridge as soon as the Indians made an appearance, and another roadblock up at the Mill Creek Road, also in the Kitwancool chiefs' territory. The Gitwangak eagles had not only held Skeena Cellulose at bay on the western frontiers, but Giila'wa was making plans for small-scale horse logging in the forests Victoria said were its own and Skeena Cellulose had planned to clearcut.

Within 24 hours after the Suskwa chiefs met that Friday in October at Gitanmaax Hall and decided to expand the territory protected by their blockade, a new roadblock camp was laid out on the tree-covered ridge above the Bulkley River, with a handful of tents and a tarpaulin-covered kitchen camp, and a roadblock bonfire was blazing on the Suskwa Main road, just north of the road's bridge across the Bulkley. By Saturday afternoon, Wet'suwet'en tribal leaders Herb and Marvin George were laughing at Gordon Sebastian's jokes at the blockade, sportsfishermen were buying $10 steelhead permits and asking the chiefs if they needed anything, children were playing in the mud puddles and the old women were cooking grouse soup in the camp.

Jack Wilson, a 56-year-old white man, part-time logger, rancher and sometime-trucker and 30-year resident of the area who lives behind the roadblock, pulled past slowly in his pickup truck after one of the boys from Gitanmaax rolled the log block out of his way. He parked his truck, walked over and warmed his hands by the fire and said he was just as happy running his 110 head of cattle on his ranch and would just as soon not have to go logging again anyway. He talked about how he hoped the government would come to the bargaining table one day, and how he understood what the chiefs were saying, and Wii Seeks assured Wilson, just in case he'd ever worried about it, that the chiefs weren't after privately held lands like the Wilson ranch. Then the talk turned to the logging, as it always does. "We selective logged in the old days," Wilson said. "There's no darn reason for those clearcuts." Wii Seeks thanked him. One of the boys passed Wii Seeks a note left for the chiefs the day before, from the Bell Pole Company, asking for access to the Itzul Creek area in order to burn landing piles and tour planting contractors to allow competitive bidding. Nobody ran for a pay phone.

Wii Seeks' cousin Vern Michell drove up on the other side of the roadblock in his Dodge Charger, handed three grouse out his window for the kitchen camp, reported formally that he saw a grizzly bear up at Mile 44, and drove off.

Ralph was quiet for a few minutes, and then he said things wouldn't be the same without his grandmother, Waigyet, but things were going to be alright. There were death feast arrangements to be made, and all the relatives would be there in Kispiox. "I'll try to carry out my responsibilities," he said, "but it will be different now that she isn't here to advise me." First it was Gwiis Gyen, Stanley Williams, the Gitwangak chief who had stood down a train in 1985 in a railway blockade. Gwiis Gyen had died in a car accident in September, at the age of 83. Waigyet was 82 when she died. They were good ages to live to, Wii Seeks said.

It started to rain, but it stopped, and the sun was out again. Mas Gak sat under a tarpaulin shelter strung between two birchpole tripods at the blockade fire. He was tired, and he hadn't been saying much. But he pointed out that the mountains just to the north, the way their ridges followed from the east to west, might put this spot on the very eastern edge of Dimlahamid.

"I think it starts here and ends up down by Gitsegukla," he said, and he recounted an old description of the city. "It took a day for a crow to fly across it. If everyone hollered, it would drop to the ground. It took place thousands of years ago. Possibly two glaciation periods ago."

He carved a circle in the muddy ground under his boots.

"I just don't think people could sustain such a big place. People were looking at whole large-sized communities, a whole bureaucratic system and a planning system to keep it in place."

And then there were the upheavals, and when the time came to go, everybody just picked up and left. Some went as far as Kitlope, some to Kemaano, some to Hartley Bay.

"Most people figure Dimlahamid is where it started, but I don't think so. That's the good part about Dimlahamid. We don't know what it means. We haven't been able to date it. I haven't been able to find a village of that size.

"What is happening is we're adjusting to what happened after Dimlahamid. The whole thing that we're doing. It's not just the management of resources apart from the management of people, eh? You're looking at a whole worldview of being part of the ecosystem, of being part of the spiritual landscape. We don't need the state. We don't need bureaucrats. We don't need police or other institutions that deny power to the people.

"The collapse of Dimlahamid reaffirms that," Mas Gak said. Then he got up, stepped around the fire to pull an axe out of a wood block and walked off to chop some more firewood.

"Let's go look around," Sebastian said, and he slapped me on the back and nodded towards his four-wheel drive. We pulled away from the camp and roared north along the dirt road towards the mountains. "They're going to have to kill him," Sebastian said, rolling down his window. The broad sweep of the Bulkley Valley in its searing autumn colours spread from the distant east to the blue-tinted high mountains ahead. All of it was now under Gitksan control. "They're probably going to have to kill him to stop him. He's just not turning back. We're not turning back.

"Hell," Sebastian said. He shifted into third and took a deep breath of the cold air pouring in his open window. "I'm going to build my house out here."

THREE

THE GHOSTS
VISIT WITH
MAS GAK

After 36 hours without sleep, Mas Gak, the man Gordon Sebastian said the enemy would probably have to kill if they wanted him stopped, sat exhausted and half asleep on a rough wooden plank. It was late Sunday night, and in the dim light of a gas lamp, with his broad shoulders hunched and his elbows on his knees, he looked up and listened. The rain hammered on the tarpaulin roof and hissed on the hot stones of the blazing campfire. He had spent the last two days cutting trees, sawing them into firewood blocks and piling them into pickup trucks. The rest of the roadblock crew built the bush camp, which consisted of a 50-foot canopy of tarpaulin, suspended from a rough frame of cottonwood beams and support poles cut from the bush along the ridge above the Bulkley. There was smoked salmon, there were foodstuffs that had been distributed at Stanley Williams' death feast, boxes of tea, coffee, canned goods, sugar, bread, sides of bacon and cartons of milk and eggs. Everything was arranged neatly on shelves constructed from sawed planks stacked on sections of tree trunks. A willow grouse hung from one pole, a huge steelhead salmon from another, and the blockade crew slept in a half-dozen tents under the canopy on the far side of the shelf wall.

Mas Gak stretched his arms, stood up slowly and stretched his back, and sat back down. And he talked about the loss of his uncle Stanley, Gwiis Gyen. Because of the slowly moving whirlpool of Gitksan names that generations of Gitksans travel through all their lives, Gwiis Gyen became Wa'Wax when he died in that car accident, Mas Gak explained. Wa'Wax had been Uncle Stanley's "baby name." It means "sleeping." With his death, the cycle of names within Gwiis Gyen's house, and within his extended family on his mother's side, was begun again, for a new generation.

In the old days, Gwiis Gyen would have been cremated, after the custom of the Gitksan and their downriver neighbours, the Tsimshian. It had been years since the last Gitksan cremation, but the language of death in this country has not changed, so that when Gwiis Gyen's fellow fireweed chiefs were calling the clans together for Uncle Stanley's death feast, at which Lorne Campbell was to inherit the name Gwiis Gyen, the chiefs did not refer to Uncle Stanley as Gwiis Gyen. They said, "We are inviting you to the cremation of Wa'Wax." Some Gitksans still burned flowers on the graves of recently dead friends, and they still burned flowers in Gitwangak, where I had visited Gwiis Gyen years earlier in his small blue house overlooking the village.

He lived there with his wife Fanny and their grandson, Clint. I remembered a painting of Christ hanging on his living room wall along with photographs of his children and a statue of the Virgin Mary on a shelf, and how the village totem poles that once faced the river were turned to face away from the river, and moved to the village park. It was in early 1986, a few weeks after Gwiis Gyen stood in front of a train on the mainline to Prince Rupert to force the Canadian National Railway to compensate the Gitwangak band for the 100 acres it took from the reserve in 1910. Back then, the line was run by the Grand Trunk Railroad. When the railway pushed through the village in 1911, it was run straight through the cemetery, and the village was given $100 to bury fourteen bodies the railwaymen disinterred.

Gitwangak is a village of about 400 people and an unknown number of ghosts. Mas Gak's memories of growing up in the old family house in the village are full of ghosts. He was never sure exactly who they were, but he knew there were many of them.

Each one had its own routine. There was the one that would walk up the old steps to the front porch and in through front door, close the door, and walk into the kitchen, and with each distinct footstep Mas Gak would hear him walking upstairs to the second floor. Sometimes the ghost would come and sit at the foot of Mas Gak's bed, and he was to speak to it, as his parents had taught him, or his mother would speak to the ghost, and eventually the ghost would get up, walk out of the room, and leave the house. Another ghost had the habit of meticulously stoking the fire in the wood-stove. First, the ghost would stoke the fire and put wood in it, then wash his hands in the wash basin in the kitchen, but it was just the sound of those things, or at least usually just sound. Sometimes the water in the wash basin would move.

Like dozens of Gitksan families, Mas Gak's family would travel to the coast in the summer to work in the salmon canneries, and one summer Mas Gak was sent back home alone to get the potato garden ready for the fall. After he had finished, he was to get back on the train and return to the coast. That night, sleeping in a main floor bedroom of the empty old house, he was awakened by sounds in the next room. They were sounds of people moving around in the room, and then the sounds of people speaking, but he couldn't make out what they were saying. He heard laughter, and the voices were becoming louder. He heard the sliding of the big board the family used to cover the top of the stairwell, and footsteps coming slowly down the stairs. Mas Gak jumped up out of bed, turned up the flame in the kerosene lamp and grabbed the .22-calibre rifle from the closet. The footsteps stopped outside his door, and Mas Gak stood there, terrified, and remembered what he had been taught about ghosts. It was wrong to be afraid, it was right to be calm, to maintain control, and to try to communicate with them. He asked, in Gitksan and then in English, "Who is it?" There was no reply.

"I have the .22 right by my leg, and when they stop right by the door I'm standing beside the door and holding it so they won't come in, and just when they get to the door they try to push the door open. I fire the .22 and I just about got my foot. The bullet landed right next to my foot."

He mustered all the courage he could, threw open the door, and ran through the kitchen. As he ran, he remembered, it was so cold in the room that it was as though a cold wind blew straight through him.

"But it was very exciting," he said. "It was communication between myself and my ancestors. I ran to my aunt's house and explained what happened. They said my ancestors were happy to see me come back and were happy with my visit and they were trying to make me comfortable.

"Those are the type of things we hear about or see all the time."

Mas Gak remembered the overgrown cremation pits from the days of his childhood in Gitwangak. Years ago, the dead chief was put in a box, and the box was placed on a pyre of logs in a pit, and the pyre was set ablaze. The body was consumed in the flames, Mas Gak said, but the heart does not burn. "I don't know," he said, when I asked him why. "The hearts just don't burn." He pushed another firelog into the flames of the campfire. "You could take a few cracks at it I guess. But they don't burn. Cremation, I think, is an interesting practice. I'd like to see that come back."

The deaths of Gwiis Gyen, and of Waigyet, the complicated arrangements for their death feasts, the grieving, the inheritance of names and the transfer of other names had overshadowed all the planning and meetings and work that went into taking this stand on the Suskwa road. It was like that with Gitksan roadblocks. The first roadblock that began the Gitksans' present campaign against outside authority — the February 1988 showdown at Little Oliver Creek — had been decided after the death feast for Johnny Mack, Klo Kumgan, one of the 54 chiefs named as plaintiffs in *Delgamuukw versus The Queen*.

Whatever it was about death feasts that charged the Gitksans' resolve, there was also a history of resistance the Gitksans could take lessons from.

The Gitksans staged what might be seen as their very first roadblock in 1872, except in this case the logging road was the Skeena River. What prompted the river blockade was the burning of Gitsegukla. The white prospectors responsible said the fire, which destroyed about a dozen communal houses and an equal number of crest poles, was an accident. A standoff resulted when the miners failed to compensate the villagers under Gitksan law. Two gunboats were sent to the mouth of the Skeena and the situation looked grim, but aboard the HMS *Scout* the Gitsegukla chiefs met with Lieutenant-Governor Joseph Trutch, where the matter was resolved to the chiefs' satisfaction. A sum of $600 was distributed as compensation among the chiefs, and with much ceremony the river blockade was lifted. The Indians fired off their muskets and sang songs, and according to reports of the day in the Victoria

Colonist, the ship's guns were fired and with the shells crashing through the trees and scudding across the water "seeming to impress the savages very forcibly with the power of the whites," the matter was concluded. The Gitksan version of events is that the chiefs were given presents as a show of goodwill, and they were compensated and treated with respect. Peace was negotiated and the river blockade was lifted.

Throughout the late nineteenth century, miners, missionaries, traders and others ventured into Gitksan territory. Their accounts clearly illustrate that the Gitksans resisted any attempts at asserting foreign authority, and the chiefs held the upper hand in relations with white authority figures. Miners and settlers were forever signing their names to petitions complaining that they were afraid for their safety and the Indians were behaving as though they owned the place. An elaborate plan to impose B.C. law on Gitksan people was devised by a certain Captain Fitzstubbs in the 1880s, who reckoned that if the Indians wouldn't obey a white man, he could give badges to the chiefs and they would uphold the Queen's law in their villages. While some chiefs apparently accepted the badges as a crude but not disagreeable form of recognized self-government, Fitzstubbs, as often as not, was laughed at. He complained that during a visit to Kispiox, the villagers were so unimpressed that "not an Indian would acknowledge my salutation." Several Kitwancool chiefs who resisted government attempts in 1927 to draw reserve boundaries around Kitwancool village were arrested and sent to jail at Oakalla prison for ripping out surveyors' stakes (Kitwancool is a fiercely independent community and its chiefs supported, but were not directly involved in, *Delgamuukw versus The Queen*). The following year, in 1928, the anthropologist Marius Barbeau wrote of Gitksan territory: "It is still an Indian country, effectively guarded — perhaps the last unconquered native stonghold of the Red Man in North America."

In many ways, that is still so, but by the 1980s the Gitksan and Wet'suwet'en people, although about 10,000 in number, were scattered throughout the west coast and outnumbered two to one by settlers in their territories. The people were poor, and they were surrounded by immigrants who knew little of their histories and often thought less of their culture. They might work alongside each other in the mills, but the white worker went home to his ranch-style bungalow in Smithers or New Hazelton and the Indian went home to his standard-federal-issue reserve house in Gitanmaax or Gitwangak. The methodology of colonialism and resistance was far more complex, and the dispossession much more thorough, but the Gitksans still had a way of getting a kick out of their end in it all.

The comical welcome Fitzstubbs encountered at Kispiox was not what federal fisheries officers were expecting when they arrived at a protest fishery on the Skeena River on July 3, 1986. The fisheries officers were sent in to enforce Ottawa's discriminatory laws against inland fisheries — laws which allocate the Gitksan and Wet'suwet'en the leavings of the Skeena and Bulkley rivers' great salmon runs after the commercial fishery has its take. It was a tense scene. The B.C. Supreme Court had just backed a coalition of commercial and sports fishing organizations against self-governing fisheries bylaws adopted by Gitksan and Wet'suwet'en villages. The B.C. government adopted the absurd position that the bylaws could apply on the reserve grounds because they were under federal jurisdiction, but the ground underneath the rivers that passed through the reserves was provincial land, so the bylaws could not apply on the rivers. That meant the Indians could fish where it was dry, but not where it was wet. So the Indians decided to go fishing, without federal permits, and when the three nervous fisheries officers approached the camp, they were pelted with marshmallows. The officers opted for a tactical retreat with plans to regroup and consult with Ottawa. Tribal council president Neil Sterritt said it was a fine defensive strategy except for the fact that some of the younger warriors kept eating all the ammunition.

Then, on April 12, 1987, 32-year-old Gitwangak band chief Glen Williams earned himself the dubious distinction of becoming the first B.C. Indian to face charges of conducting an illegal bingo. The B.C. Bingo Hall Owners Association was concerned about Indian bingo, and the B.C. attorney-general's department ordered RCMP spies to Gitksan bingo games to gather intelligence on one of the few methods of fund-raising the Gitksan and Wet'suwet'en reserves had available to them. Williams built an elementary school in Gitwangak with "illegal" bingo funds, and the revenue helped pay off the mortage on the tribal council office in Hazelton. Bingo players came from as far away as Saskatchewan to join in one of the Gitksans' legendary "monster" bingos, prizes were often in the tens of thousands of dollars, and one local Gitksan won himself a brand new Pontiac Grand Am with a $500 insurance certificate and a full tank of gas. Bingo came easy to the Gitksan and Wet'suwet'en, since it was little more than a complicated version of the old lahal games and bone-gambling tournaments (Gitksan elders routinely save their money for trips to the Nevada gambling casinos of Las Vegas and Reno). But every time a Gitksan was charged and mounted a challenge on aboriginal rights, the B.C. attorney-general's office backed off, reckoning the government would lose because of the shaky ground it stood on.

It was important to keep a sense of humour about all of this. But it wasn't easy.

The campfire flames hissed in the rain and Mas Gak reflected on the years that had brought him to the camp on that dark, wooded bluff above the Bulkley. His wife Sheila was back at the house in Two Mile, just above Hazelton, wondering when he was coming home. In Ottawa, Indian Affairs Minister Pierre Cadieux was considering his advisors' reports about the situation that was developing so many thousands of miles away and about how to take a position that did not inflame the Indians or enrage B.C.'s white politicians. In Victoria, Indian Affairs Minister Jack Weisgerber considered the political implications of the choices in front of him, the options he would have to consider as soon as he walked into his legislative offices on the coming Monday morning, with meetings to make and calls to return from the attorney-general's office with its reports from the Hazelton RCMP substation, the forest ministry and its reports from Westar Timber and logging contractors, and the calls from news reporters.

For Mas Gak, the implications of uncontrolled development in the Gitksan and Wet'suwet'en territories were more stark, and they returned to him easily in the faces of the foster children, the battered wives, the incest victims and the alcoholics that so many Indian people had become. During his years as a social worker, he had seen those faces, scattered from Prince Rupert to Terrace, from Burns Lake to Vancouver. They were the walking remnants of proud familes, of houses with ancient histories and titles of great nobility.

Between 1961 and 1973, a time of great social collapse in Indian communities across the west, more than 4,000 native Indian children in British Columbia were apprehended by social workers and placed in white foster homes. There was a market for them, and the communities from which they were taken had little or no power to hold on to them. As Mas Gak sat on the sawn plank bench of the kitchen camp that night, a third of the roughly 6,000 children "in care" in the province, either in foster homes or in youth detention centres or in some other way a ward of the state, were still Indian children. Thousands more had been adopted by loving and well-meaning white families, or were trying to make their way through the world as adults, not knowing who they were or where they came from or why they were taken in the first place.

"I think the whole experience as a social worker certainly influenced me in what I saw was one of the major problems that we had," said Mas Gak, who adopted Wayne, a thirteen-year-old Kispiox wolf, in 1971. "I could see the problems we had there, just the whole attitude of society in regards to being capable of being in care of children. People just didn't have any idea of the traditional system we had. A lot of the family breakdown, and the biggest places where I saw the isolation of the families, was when they left the community here and they ended up in either Burns Lake or Smithers or Terrace or Rupert or the big urban centres. But you could really see the total collapse of that whole network where we were losing those kids."

One of those kids was a troubled boy with a heart defect, born in 1967 with fetal alcohol syndrome and an addiction to heroin. In 1986, Billy Rodgers died on the cold, concrete floor of an underground parking garage in New Westminster, hundreds of miles away from his home. He never knew it, but he was the grandson of a Gitksan hereditary chief, and was entitled by Gitksan law to a privileged place in the feast house, fishing stations on the Skeena River, hunting areas and traplines in the mountains above Gitsegukla. He was also unaware that he was the subject of a desparate search by his extended family that began shortly after he was born. The family pleaded with social services officials to let them get in touch with him, but following policy, the government said no. Billy had been taken from his alcoholic mother at the age of eight days and placed in a white foster home over the protests of his grandmother, 79-year-old Maria Jackson, who had obtained custody of his two brothers and two sisters.

Despite years of attempts, Maria and Billy's oldest sister, Sharon Russell, could not convince the social services ministry to tell them where Billy was. But around the time that Wii Seeks was standing down Wester Timber during the final days of the Babine River campaign at Sam Green Creek, provincial officials wrote to Sharon in Gitsegukla to say they would help her find Billy. By the time the B.C. Appeals Court ruled in a two-to-one decision against Westar Timber's plans to build a bridge across the Babine, Sharon Russell got another letter from Victoria telling her Billy was dead. The coroner's inquiry states: "On Feb. 23, 1986, at approximately 0900 hours, William Edward Vanderhoef [his adopted name], aged 18 years, was found lying lifeless on the floor of a basement parking lot in the New Westminster area. He was lying on his back, and found in his hand was a short piece of garden hose." The report concluded that the boy had died of sudden cardiac arrythmia, caused by inhaling gasoline to produce euphoria.

Mas Gak knew first hand how the process of apprehension worked, because it used to be his job.

"I found it so easy to take kids away from their families," he said, sitting with his hands tucked in his jacket pockets in the dim light of the campfire and the gas lamps of the kitchen camp. "That was the easiest thing for me as a social worker, to get court orders that committed the child to the superintendent of child welfare, for life. In some cases all you had to do was get the documents all set up and put out a notice in the paper and if nobody responded, you went into court and you just processed all these forms, and the next thing you had all these kids on your hands.

"That was hard for me when I started working in Vancouver. I saw all that, where young mothers had given up their babies at the hospital, and we used to have to wait ten days to finalize the decision with the mother. And then picking up the babies, picking them all up at the hospital, and then taking them to court and identifying them all, and then giving them names and processing the documents and sending them to receiving homes. Mary, Joe, Pete, Bill, whatever. You had to make up your mind before you got to family court down on the waterfront there."

In his own childhood, Mas Gak was spared the confinement of residential schools and foster homes, but much of his youth was spent away from Gitksan territory. In the village of Gitwangak there was no high school, and Indian Affairs education authorities sent Indian children to be billetted wherever they could find a high school with a family willing to take one. He went to school in Prince Rupert and Port Simpson, and one September morning, Mas Gak got on a bus in Prince Rupert with an Indian Affairs bus ticket and instructions to tell the bus driver to stop at Brown Road in Langley, hundreds of miles away in the Fraser Valley. The family met him at the crossroads. He stayed with several families, United Church members, Anglicans and Baptists, went to high school in Langley, Abbotsford and Aldergrove, went on to college and Simon Fraser University, earning credits towards a degree in business administration and a diploma in social work along the way. When he came home, he knew exactly what he had to do.

"When I got back here, I got into all of that right off the bat. Writing letters, trying to find out where the kids were, why they were taken, piecing together the history of that family, locating them in foster homes, working with other social workers, trying to make the connection with the kids down in the Lower Mainland and the grandparents up here. It was really sad. Just to turn that around and get that going, I think that was all part of the whole exercise of changing my opinion of where we were going."

After taking two years off to travel the world, Mas Gak

came home convinced that a total restoration of the traditional system was the only solution. The old system was still
there, but the band council structures and the tribal council
structures had to be dismantled, restoring the authority of the
hereditary chiefs and asserting that authority on the land.

It meant abandoning the city-state, with all its bureaucracy,
its boom-and-bust economics, its child-welfare superinten-
dents, its police and its reserves. It meant returning to an
integrated whole, a worldview that connected the dead with
the living, the animals with the people, the laws of the earth
with the laws of society. For the Gitksan and Wet'suwet'en, it
meant a return to a society based on matrilineal clans, each
comprised of houses, or wilps, and within each wilp a chief,
whose duties to his wilp members was also his authority over
them. Each chief and wilp was inextricably linked by ancient
history to a territory of land, and the chief owned the territory in the same way the territory owned the chief.

Sitting in the dark on that wet sawn plank, as the fire was
finally growing cold from the heavy rains, Mas Gak yawned
and looked around him. By morning, in Hazelton, there
would be telephone calls from police and politicians and
bureaucrats and reporters from hundreds and thousands of
miles away, everybody wanting to know what this latest
roadblock was all about, how much territory was now within
the chiefs' total control, how many sawmill jobs would be
threatened if this kept up and what it would take to bring the
roadblock down.

In Gitksan country, there were people who were concerned about where Mas Gak's strategy was going. He was
taking his instructions from the chiefs, but there were some
who weren't totally convinced. And there were others who
saw the war on the land as their last hope, their last stand.
Many of the older people who were with Mas Gak and Wii

Seeks understood the old medicines and had been using them to look after Mas Gak and Wii Seeks. Among them were members of Mas Gak's extended family. They used herbs, and colour, and light, and Mas Gak was sure they were aware of his health and his emotional state from miles and miles away.

"They spend a lot of their time helping me," Mas Gak said. "They have to. They have to make sure. They have to make sure I don't ... lose it. A lot of the work that people want done isn't finished, and a lot of the ideas we've got haven't been tested yet. So the work we've been doing now I think is just the beginning of what's to come, and if we don't finish it, or I'm not involved in it, then I'm finished."

He sat quietly and stared at the ground.

"I'm finished."

FOUR

IN THE STREETS
OF AN
ANCIENT CITY

'Noola was the last chief to leave Dimlahamid.

The seasons had turned back upon themselves, and the city's final punishment began. The arc of the sun ended its northward migration and turned back again to the south. With each new morning, the snowline crept further down the mountainsides until the snow began to fall in the streets of Dimlahamid.

The people of the great city had grown insolent and careless. They failed to honour the remains of the first returning salmon of spring. First, Gyaren mocked the sky with the first salmon's bones, and then the people noticed red squirrels running across the salmon weirs. The skies darkened, and the snow fell, and it kept falling until all the great houses in Dimlahamid disappeared beneath it.

After thousands had starved to death or abandoned the city forever, the bluejay Kwiskwas landed at the edge of the smokehole in the roof of 'Noola's house, and the chief saw that somewhere the seasonal cycle had not collapsed, that somewhere it was spring. Throughout Dimlahamid, the dead lay in the snowbound tombs their houses had become, but with their hopes renewed by Kwiskwas, 'Noola's people began a tunnel, following the chief Tawee-welp, and the half starved survivors made their way out of Dimlahamid up the Skeena River, and settled near a small canyon.

One day quietly passed into the next.

In Victoria, Indian Affairs Minister Jack Weisgerber and deputy minister Eric Denhoff were meeting with Attorney-General Bud Smith to talk about the Gitksan roadblocks. In Hazelton, contractor Brian Larson wondered if and when he'd be able to get his crews back on that thinning contract up in the Suskwa. At Carnaby, Westar's Keith Spencer told his men he didn't know how many days were left before the Gitwangak mill would run out of wood, and the mill needed timber that was behind a Gitksan roadblock up at the Mill Creek Road. The company had planned to move back into the Suskwa area before the month was out, but now there was no telling what would happen. At Two Mile, Kispiox forest district manager Charlie Willson waited for instructions from Victoria, but none came. In New Hazelton, Dave Webster from Dee-Jay Contracting reckoned he had three weeks' work left before the roadblocks started slowing things down for him, too.

At the Bulkley River bridge, the occasional steelhead fisherman drove up to the roadblock bonfire on the Suskwa road and paid his ten dollars for a one-day fishing permit and stopped back at the bonfire to show off what he'd caught or talk about the one that he didn't catch. The few families that lived in the aspen-and-cottonwood bottomlands behind the roadblock slowed their pickup trucks and waved as they came and went along the muddy road, and nobody seemed to mind much.

Wendall Bragg suspected some sinister hand behind the

roadblocks, but he wasn't quite sure whose hand it was. Chris Atkins said he didn't mind the roadblock and he was all in favour of a land claims settlement as long as it didn't affect his property values. Kenny Rabnett, a homesteader who lived with his goats, horses and chickens deep in the bush at the head of the old Babine Trail, was a longtime supporter of the chiefs, and he told anyone who cared to ask that he thought it was a great idea that they were standing up to the forest companies. Brenda Forsyth said it didn't bother her any, except when there was that mixup about whether they could haul wood off their own property, but other than that everything seemed to be okay by her. They all clattered by in their pickup trucks, carrying on with their lives, breaking the monotony of the bonfire.

Then there was old Tom Atrill, who seemed to spend most of his days brooding about the state of the world from his peculiar "second-hand store" down a dirt road a few miles in from the bridge. He had a column in the local newspaper and it made him a bit of a redneck celebrity. He railed against the malcontent French and the upstart Indians and how the world was headed in a handbasket in the general direction of hell. Atrill reckoned that the Indians at the roadblock didn't have the authority to ask him so much as the time of day, and after the blockade went up, he headed straight for the RCMP substation in Hazelton with demands that the Mounties uphold the law, but the sergeant more or less told him to go home and keep his opinions to himself. So he busied himself with letters to the prime minister and offered his views to customers who came to buy a used car or a piece of a used car or just to look and see what he had acquired since their last visit.

Mas Gak and Wii Seeks and Herb and Marvin George carried on the tribal council's affairs on fax machines and telephones and in meeting rooms and offices, and the hereditary chiefs carried on with the business of life and death. There was Fanny Morrison's stone feast to be seen to. It was a gathering to feast for the raising of a headstone, a modern equivalent of a pole-raising feast. Fanny had died twenty years earlier, but her son Willie was never quite settled about his responsibilities in completing the cycle of fireweed feasts for her, and it had been bothering him all these years. And there was the feast for Lelt, the late Fred Johnson of Gitwangak. And there was another feast in Kispiox, the death feast for Mabel White. And there was much planning and arranging to be done for the feast for Wii Seeks' grandmother Waigyet, Elsie Morrison.

On this particular morning, the roadblock bush camp was quiet and the mountains were dark and still. The initial excitement of setting it up had passed, and all the chiefs were gone but 'Noola. 'Noola sat on a frost-covered plank beside the campfire on the wooded ridge above the Bulkley River as the world outside went about its business. After the countless death feasts since the fall of the Gitksans' great city, 'Noola, the last chief in Dimlahamid, was now 39-year-old Norman Moore, who also held the name Hleegam Genx, Where It Is Worn Out, which refers to a particular habit of the grizzly bear, which is to wear out a trail over succeeding generations of bears passing the same way as they make their seasonal rounds. 'Noola was a big man with thick black hair, from a poor family of eight brothers and two sisters who grew up in a small house upriver from Gitanmaax. One of his brothers, Lester Moore, was Xsimwits'iin, one of the senior chiefs with territory behind the Suskwa roadblock, and it was in Xsimwits'iin's wilp, or house, that 'Noola now sat. His mother, the frog clan matriarch Spaa'last, worked in the kitchen at the Hazelton hospital to help raise her family. 'Noola's father was Laats, of the wolf clan, in the house of

Wii K'aax. Laats had been a logger. 'Noola hadn't had a job worth talking about for years.

The flap opened on a frost-covered tent on the far side of the tarpaulin-covered kitchen camp and out crawled Ernie Muldoe, Haa'txw, 'Noola's maternal uncle. Ernie had made a home for himself in his small tent at the bush camp. It contained just about all the worldly possessions he had acquired during his 68 years, mostly clothes and assorted gear, stacked neatly in the cramped corners around his sleeping bag inside. Haa'txw warmed himself by the fire and held his cup of morning coffee in both his hands. In a torn toque, a tattered coat and woollen pants, he had only just come home from Sacramento where he had spent years living in the farmworker camps of California's central valley, working in the fields alongside Mexicans. He was here because he had nowhere else to go.

And so we sat and drank coffee and tried to wake up, and took to skinning the grouse Soup Wilson had shot for us the day before. 'Noola started on the blue grouse, Ernie started on the fool hen and I got to work on the willow grouse.

It was about that time that Soup and Josh woke up.

Soup Wilson, a 49-year-old Gitksan frog, walked over to the campfire, and Josh McLean, a 59-year-old Gitksan wolf, followed behind. They both sat down for a minute, then they both got up, walked slowly to the plank table, found two clean cups and walked back to the fire. Soup pulled the coffee kettle from the side of the fire, filled his cup, and emptied the rest into the cup Josh held out to him.

The five of us exchanged good mornings.

Soup and Josh both wear red and black mackinaw jackets. Josh wears a mackinaw cap and Soup, whose real name is Joe, wears a Husqvarna baseball cap. Both are trappers, and they're seldom far apart from one another. Both were badly injured in the forest industry, and both have scraped by with low-key and occasional thinning jobs from contractors like Brian Larson's outfit ever since they got hurt. For Soup, the end of his career as a faller came when a tree fell on him and cracked the bones in the back of his neck, and he's got a plastic disk between the two top vertebrae. Josh got hurt back in 1975 when the crew van he was riding in got hit by a logging truck and his legs got smashed. And he can't handle a power saw of any size now without his hands swelling up.

Both were working on a thinning contract with Larson's crew before the first Suskwa roadblock went up and shut the job down, so now they were out of work, too, like 'Noola and Haa'txw. But they didn't complain, and they seemed to be enjoying themselves. "Long as they feed me," Soup used to say. "Long as they feed me, too," Josh would answer. Chances were good that they would be feeding the camp as often as not. Soup did shoot the grouse we were skinning, after all.

"The heads we save for the special guest," 'Noola said. He looked at Soup and Josh and pointed at me. Haa'txw smiled. I looked at the blue grouse's head at 'Noola's feet. Its left eye stared at me.

"Oh. Really."

"I'm kidding," he said. He laughed to himself. "Don't worry."

It was a cold and quiet morning, like a lot of mornings in the camp. The place had begun to take on its own routines while the world outside carried on with its affairs. There was breakfast, woodcutting, hunting for grouse or moose, lunch, fishing for steelhead, dinner, shifts at the roadblock, hours sitting at the fire in camp and maybe some time away in town, either at Suzanne's Deli in New Town, the Inlander Hotel cafe in Old Town or a bingo somewhere. Sgenna would come by and stand guard at the roadblock, or lean over the bridge railing and fire his revolver at an imaginary target in the river below while Yagosip, his wife, cooked lunch and told stories about picking huckleberries along the railroad tracks when she was a child. Yagosip and Sgenna had spent much of the first few days of the first Suskwa roadblock alone, and Sgenna's knee was acting up again. But there was always someone dropping by with boxes of bread or some bags of coffee or cartons of milk and packages of chocolate wagonettes. At night, the squirrels called to one another through the trees, the Bulkley River continued its quiet roar below the wooded ridge and the trains passed through the dark hills on the far side of river, carrying grain from the prairies east to saltwater at Prince Rupert for the markets across the Pacific.

On this particular morning, like many mornings in the bush camp, there was 'Noola and Haa'txw, Soup, Josh, and me.

"Dimlahamid is a really old place," 'Noola said, as he tugged off another handful of grouse feathers. "Thousands of years ago. Once you could still see where 'Noola's house was. It's just upriver from Gitanmaax. That's where Neil Sterritt's farm is.

"It's interesting. It was one of the largest of the houses in the area. I guess 'Noola, years ago, covered a lot of territory, but his house started to disperse because there were too many people in the house. It was about a hundred years ago that 'Noola was the head chief of all the frog clan in this area. Now, I'm living in my brother's house, Xsimwits'iin's house. And my name hasn't risen again to the status that it should be. It's called 'to complete the work that has to be done.' I'm not sure what I will do. I think I will have to raise a pole.

"At Dimlahamid, 'Noola was the head man there. His house was the only house that was dug into the ground. You walk into the house and it's straight down, and then another tier and it's straight down, and that's where the chief was. He was the head chief of the house then, and it was just a hundred years ago that he was the head frog chief in Gitanmaax, but 'Noola's name started to decline, and Xsimwits'iin started to become the main chief. Ludkudzii Wus is in that house. It was Xsimwits'iin that put up that pole when Tom Campbell died. He died in 1945. He had both names, Ludkudzii Wus and Xsimwits'iin. Tom Campbell had a sister and her name was Lucy Muldoe, and she had the name 'Noola. Women had that name and that's why it dropped a little bit, I guess. It started during the depression."

Ludkudzii Wus and Xsimwits'iin. Ludkudzii Wus was now old Ben Mackenzie, not exactly in the best of health, but in his clearer moments he could spin yarns about packing the mail by horse on the old trail to Fort Babine. And Xsimwits'iin was Lester Moore.

"We are a very traditional family, our family, and we never lost our traditions," 'Noola went on. "Where we grew up is in the feast house. Our parents and grandparents taught us all the laws, the taboo laws, the feast laws and the respect laws. We don't look our elders in the face and some white people don't understand, when we're showing respect. They think we're being unmannerly, but we're showing respect."

He looked me in the eye. "I'm starting to lose that a little bit." He laughed again.

"In the old days, people went where they could live off the land," 'Noola said, "where there were trees in the wintertime, that they could use for firewood. They built their houses, and after ten or twenty years, they would move to another part of their territory. There were places they would go every summer, to harvest the fish, and you have to survive, eh? You don't stay where you can't live. In those days, they migrated over the land, and of course they had their places where they met, and they had their feasts. One place is where Gitanmaax is now. White people, the government, didn't know that it was a meeting place where all the people would meet. They would have feasts and everything."

And in all the Gitksan sagas, told and retold down through the generations, lamented in songs, re-enacted in masked dances and carved in totem poles, the greatest feasting place of all was Dimlahamid, or Dizkle, that long-abandoned city that has confounded archeologists for more than 60 years, and still remains unfound.

As early as 1915, anthropologist Edward Sapir had concluded that whatever Dimlahamid was, and wherever it was, it was clear that the clan system, so deeply rooted in the cultures of the North Pacific coast, originated in distinct, animal-named hunting bands that gathered at Dimlahamid, or Dizkle, or whatever it was, and later established themselves over hundreds of thousands of square miles of coastal forests, mountains and river valleys. The extent and elaboration of the Gitksan "myth" of Dimlahamid was recorded for the outside world as early as 1923, when a local amateur anthropologist, Constance Cox, learned of it from Kam Ya'en, a fireweed chief from Gitsegukla. Archeologist Harlan Smith searched for it in the 1920s, and so did the pioneer anthropologists Marius Barbeau and Diamond Jenness. They found no evidence of this metropolis on the Skeena, no evidence of any city on the Bulkey. The National Museum of Man sent a survey crew through the area in 1966 and no remains of any city were found. Through the 1970s, more researchers combed the hills and valley bottoms from Gitsegukla to Moricetown and came back empty.

By the time *Delgamuukw versus The Queen* had begun its weary voyage through the court system, archeologist Sylvia Albright had concluded in an exhaustive inventory of known "prehistoric sites" in the Gitksan and Wet'suwet'en territories that in spite of the years of fruitless searches, the archeological record essentially confirms the oral histories of the Gitksan ada'ox and Wet'suwet'en kungax. Each "story," if it can be called that, is "owned" by particular clan houses and the chiefs that govern them. And when a chief recounts a story, Albright found, the story can generally be confirmed by physical evidence. The time frames also correspond, and evidence of village settlements and cache pits have been found in the vicinity of Dizkle that reach back 6,000 years, and in the adjacent vicinity of Dimlahamid, 5,000 years. If a story within the Gitksan ada'ox recounts the presence of, say, an ancestral village inhabited at about the time of Dimlahamid, such as Gitangasx on the Upper Skeena, Albright would find it, or something associated with it. Several Gitksan houses own stories relating to ancestors at Gitangasx, and those stories led her to several food cache pits in the vicinity of the site where Gitangasx is said to have been. As early as the 1920s, the general correlation of the Wet'suwet'en kungax and documentable evidence was presumed to be a good place to start looking for Dizkle, and Jenness poked around a heavily wooded area that had been a section of Dizkle the Wet'suwet'en Thin House people recall as Hawilamax (Place Where People Throw Away Turnips). He found no evidence of a city, but he did find wild turnips growing there. Albright listened to Gitksan chiefs' accounts from the ada'ox that describe the Upper Skeena village of Kisgegas as a major town that was the centre of several tributary villages centuries earlier, and she found archeological evidence of several surrounding villages in the vicinity of Kisgegas and a large food storage area "containing at least 230 cache pits, [indicating] intensive exploitation and processing of local resources by a population occupying permanent winter villages in the area."

The city of Dimlahamid itself, Albright suggests, is in fact a general locality of several major towns. The Gitksan ada'ox contains accounts of several towns or boroughs in the immediate area, such as Anwaris (Place of Digging), Dimlahamid proper (On Fine Prairie), Gwetset, Angudoon, Gwenrald (Sandhill Crane), Kunradal and Keemalay. The "stories" associated with each place are elaborate, instructive and dramatic, and the mere names of each town serve a function in and of themselves, like the title of a story or the mask on a dancer. Anwaris refers to the story of a man who lost his child, and went nearly mad with grief. He kept hearing the child crying, and he believed the voice to be coming from underground. He began to dig, and he dug holes throughout the town. The crying stopped during the daylight hours, and the townsfolk, taking pity on the man, consulted a wise woman, who said simply that the night had taken the baby from its father. The story concludes with the townspeople being struck with a vision of a man standing on the moon, carrying a bucket, and that's why Anwaris had that name. Some names are almost stories in themselves, as in Angudoon, which is translated as The Steep Place On the Riverbank Where a Man Is Pulled Up With the Right Hand Of a Friend.

But the most dramatic and often-told stories about Dimlahamid, the stories that are most central to the Gitksan way of seeing the world, are the stories about the various punishments visited upon the city and its eventual abandonment, when 'Noola looked up to see Kwiskwas sitting on the edge of the smokehole of his nearly buried house so many centuries earlier. And if the archeological record shows anything dramatic, it is a consistency with the Gitksan ada'ox related to the punishment of Dimlahamid, or at least a clear and strangely precise record of a sudden change in the way people lived, and where they lived, throughout the entire northwest region of Canada, about 3,500 years ago. But it still shows no city.

The story of Dimlahamid would probably fill a library, but

the most succinct and complete account comes from Ken Harris, a high-ranking Gitksan chief who carries the exalted name Hagbegwatku. In 1948, Harris persuaded his uncle, Arthur McDames, to allow him to record his stories about the city. Harris' mother helped him translate the stories, which were published by the University of B.C. in 1974 as *Visitors Who Never Left*. There are voluminous references to events in and around Dimlahamid, or versions of similar narratives related to Dimlahamid, in almost every Gitksan chief's personal ada'ox, and many have been written in English and recorded among the literary possessions of individual chiefs in the library of the Office of the Gitksan and Wet'suwet'en Hereditary Chiefs in Hazelton. The narratives are property, and cannot be recreated with any great effectiveness (in print, anyway, removed from their appropriate context). There are many variant stories throughout the Tsimshian-speaking area, belonging to various chiefs within different houses and different clans, and the accounts vary in subtle ways from narrative to narrative, but a certain identifiable history of the place emerges.

To the extent that it has a beginning and an end, the story of Dimlahamid begins, for the Gitksan fireweed clan at least, in the sky.

In a dispute that began with the violation of a taboo law governing the hunt, the people of Kunradal attack and kill everyone in the village of Keemalay except Abalone-Pearl-Labret and her daughter, Skawah, who hide from the invaders. After wandering through the forests, hoping to find a husband for her daughter and a means to avenge the destruction of Keemalay, Abalone-Pearl-Labret eventually marries Skawah to Sunbeams, son of the chief of the sky, and then Skawah's mother, at the point of death, instead becomes forever the sound the wind makes as it passes through the forest. Skawah lives among the sky people and bears Sunbeams several children, and Sunbeams' father gives the children names, powers, and instructions with which they are to return to earth. These gifts are embodied in the first crests (the sun, the moon and the stars), the first totem pole, an earthquake charm contained in a magic basket, and explicit directions regarding a variety of subjects from the treatment of animals to the construction of houses. The sky children become the first fireweed people and they settle on earth, the Kunradal people are punished, and the new people multiply among the earthborn and swell the human population, forming the vast city-state of Dimlahamid.

It is not long before the people of Dimlahamid become reckless and abandon the sky chief's instructions. These stories begin with a group of children who use a bear's stomach as a football. A white feather falls from the sky, and one morning shortly thereafter the children awake to find the bones of the grown-ups of Dimlahamid scattered throughout the countryside. The children are repentant, and they are given powers to revive the dead, but some of the skeletal remains are not reconstructed properly, and many of the people become cripples. But Dimlahamid is given another chance.

The years pass, the city once again flourishes, and the men travel far afield to take trophies of mountain goat heads, again violating the law. On one hunting trip, six cousins slaughter an entire herd of the great white-coated goats and make games with their horns. In one story, the hero is Hagbeg-watku, in another it is Du'as. The young man befriends a goat kid that somehow survived the massacre, marks it with red ochre and sets it free. The months pass, and a company of strangers arrives at Dimlahamid to invite the people to a great feast. The strangers sleep on the grass and hide their faces when they are eating until the time comes to lead the people of Dimlahamid to their village, and the procession travels up the slopes of Stegyawden, now known as Mount Rocher

DeBoule, the great craggy peak overlooking the broad valleys at the confluence of the Skeena and the Bulkley rivers. The feast begins, and a great drama ensues. A supernatural one-horned mountain goat appears as the chief of the feast hosts, and thousands of the visitors from Dimlahamid fall to their deaths down the mountainside. The goat kid, with its ochre-painted face, saves the young man who had befriended him, and the survivor returns to tell the few remaining residents of Dimlahamid what the city had brought upon itself.

Again, Dimlahamid recovers, and the years pass. This time, the rains fall, and it rains for a year. The surface of the water is covered in the feathers of exhausted birds who find nowhere to rest. Thousands perish, but those who had remained loyal to the instructions of the chief of the sky had constructed their houses in the appropriate way, and the houses float, anchored by long ropes made of hide, cedar bark and roots. Eventually the waters subside, the survivors build up the city again and an age of great prosperity and peace follows.

The last great catastrophe, before the final snowfall, occurs in the saga of the Medeek, a ferocious spirit sometimes associated with the grizzly bear and sometimes with the mountain lion. It is a story of a great ecological upheaval that occurred in the vicinity of Dimlahamid about 3,500 years ago. One account begins with a company of young women at the Lake of the Summer Pavilions, now known as Seeley Lake, near Carnaby in the hills south of the Skeena River. The women assemble there to fish for trout, gather berries and practice songs and dances for the elaborate theatrical performances that the Gitksan traditionally engaged in during the winter months. One summer, a woman fashions a headdress from trout bones, and her friends follow her example. After some years, the people of Angudoon in Dimlahamid are shaken by a great commotion deep in the forest on the south side of the river, where a small creek empties into the Skeena from the Lake of the Summer Pavilions. Trees are uprooted and thrown skyward as some supernatural force makes its way down the creek towards the riverbank. The Medeek appears on the opposite shore, gazes out upon Dimlahamid and crosses the river. An epic battle ensues. River levels rise and fall, mountainsides crumble, and the battle continues along the Street of Chiefs. The Medeek destroys everything in his path, and is eventually driven back into the Skeena River. He makes his way back through the forest, and disappears again beneath the waters of Seeley Lake.

In *Delgamuukw versus The Queen*, the provincial government dismisses the Gitksan ada'ox as a mere collection of folk tales. This assessment may not have occurred to geologist Allen Gottesfeld in 1985 when he was conducting a survey in the area of Chicago Creek, which drains Seeley Lake and empties into the Skeena. Gottesfeld found that about 3,500 years ago, massive debris torrents roared down the creek canyon, smashing through the forest and uprooting trees as it went. In November 1986, Simon Fraser University professor Rolf Mathewes obtained core samples from the sediment at the bottom of Seeley Lake. What he found was that a great ecological upheaval had occurred at about the same time the Medeek rose from the lake, and radiocarbon dates showed it took place about 3,500 years ago. The lake level rose six feet and fell again, hillsides cascaded into gullies and creeks changed their courses.

From these events, the Gitksan chiefs have obtained some of the most precious contents of their ada'ox. But the ada'ox represents more than mere fanciful accounts of geological and botanical phenomena, although it certainly does provide hard evidence of an elaborate Gitksan society that reaches back in time beyond the days of ancient Greece. The ada'ox defines the land as much as the land defines the ada'ox. And as for the people, the ada'ox determines where you sit in the feast house, what symbols may appear on the robes you wear, and what images are carved into your mortuary pole.

The ada'ox is not something for which there is an easy translation into the English language, because it consists of stories, but it also consists of maps, genealogies, heraldry, social morality and art. It is both philosophy and private property.

It doesn't translate well into Canadian law, either, and in accepting ada'ox in evidence, B.C. Supreme Court Judge Allan McEachern had to bend the hearsay rule in a procedure he described as "almost unknown to our law." It hasn't been easy for the chiefs, either. Because the B.C. government forced the Gitksan and Wet'suwet'en to prove their very existence in court, the chiefs had to symbolically open and display the contents of their ada'ox. For some chiefs, the demand has been extremely difficult, as it was for Art Matthews, a 47-year-old sawfiler at the Gitwangak sawmill who is also the house chief Tenimgyet of the Gitksan wolves. It took him eight trial days in the courtroom at the Robson Square courthouse in downtown Vancouver to recount some of the contents of the ada'ox he is personally responsible for by virtue of his name. One "chapter" of his ada'ox, which includes an account of a young woman kidnapped by grizzly bears in the mountains northeast of Gitwangak, provides instructions in hunting methods and conservation rules. Tenimgyet was obliged to recite those stories and explain their meaning. At the end of those eight days, he was exhausted and angry. At the close of the last day, in an office the chiefs had rented across the street from the courthouse, he hosted an impromptu feast, consisting of dried seaweed, blueberries, oolichan grease and Kentucky Fried Chicken. He wanted to ceremonially close the symbolic bent-cedar box that contained his ada'ox as soon as possible, get out of Vancouver and get back home.

To the Gitksan, their very identities derive from the ada'ox. Their names, songs, social responsibilities, crests and political status derive from the animals, the people, events, supernatural forces and natural forces that occur in the ada'ox — one-horned goats, strange bear spirits, rainbows, skeletons scattered in the streets of an ancient city and young girls dancing at the Lake of the Summer Pavilions. And it is an earthquake charm, the sound the wind makes when it passes through the trees, and a bluejay that sits at the edge of a smokehole as the snow falls and covers all the houses.

"Coming?"

It had taken me a lot longer than I thought it would to clean all the feathers from the willow grouse. I had dozed off, but the grouse was naked at my feet. I looked up to see Soup Wilson standing with his rifle in front of the fire.

"Well? Coming?"

"Sure," I said.

And so we headed out for the high country with Soup at the wheel of his old van and Josh in the back rolling Player's tobacco from a can balanced on his knee into thin cigarettes twirled with one hand.

"We'll get some steelhead tomorrow," Soup said, pulling out from the dirt track that leads into the bush camp and out onto the Suskwa road. Soup got some more fish eggs from Robert Jackson the day before, and he said that's all he'd need, and I remembered when Herb George and I headed up to a bend in the Suskwa River where Herb said he'd never been skunked. We expected to catch anything we went after, decked out in all our high-tech flyfishing gear, but we came back empty, and later that day Soup headed out with a bent hook and some tangled fishing line and those eggs Jackson gave him and came back with three steelhead.

You guys weren't fishing in the right place, I guess, he had said, charitably. If Soup says we'll catch steelhead tomorrow, we'll catch steelhead tomorrow. This morning we're after more grouse.

We waved to 'Noola and Haa'txw at the roadblock bonfire and headed off. In the rear view mirror I watched them as they sat there staring into the fire. They got smaller with every bump and pothole. To the east, the snow was creeping further down the mountainsides with each passing day.

A few miles up, we stopped and headed into the bush after a willow grouse we spooked from the road. We followed him into some underbrush and for a second I thought I had him between the rifle crosshairs but he spooked again. No luck. He's gone. Soup made a remark about having me along, and how it must be that I've been with a woman too recently, or something like that.

We got back in the van and headed north in the sleet, the forest growing darker and more green with hemlock, cedar and spruce. The narrow road through the Suskwa high country snakes through the trees and under black cliff faces. It was like moving through darkened halls, and the road continues like this all the way to the Babine River, where Westar had hoped for that new bridge to end-run the territory sealed off by Wii Seeks and the others at the Sam Green Creek blockade in the summer. Now Westar was shut out of these mountains, too, and the mood in Hazelton and New Hazelton and South Hazelton and Carnaby was getting a little grim.

Lots of porcupine up here, Soup remarked. The road wound its way through gloomy mountains hunched shoulder to shoulder with thick black clouds.

We were leaving Dimlahamid now, into the country of the goats, and the snow was getting heavier.

E L S I E   M O R R I S O N ' S
D E A T H   F E A S T

After the great snowfall buried Dimlahamid, Wii Seeks and his fireweed people, the people of the sky, travelled west. His party of canoes travelled down the seacoast, where the flotilla passed the homes of many sea monsters, but the people failed to provide them with offerings of mountain goat fat as a sign of respect. Reaching a place known for its dangerous whirlpools, at what is now Point Lambert, just below Port Essington, the lead canoe was pulled beneath the waves so violently that the tow rope to a following canoe was snapped. At that point, a creature arose from the waves, a creature with a man's body and a woman's face, and the creature sang a dirge.

The following canoe was swept up an arm of the Skeena River and settled at a place near the point where the Canadian National Railway built its Sockeye station about 3,000 years later. The night the canoe landed there an old woman in the party had a vision of men building a house, and on the front of the house a whirlpool was painted. Inside the house the man-woman monster sat among paintings of sea urchins and other saltwater creatures, and the men sang dirges. The woman's vision is the source of the crests held by Wii Seeks, which literally translated means "big splash," and the dirges became Wii Seeks' property.

By the time I arrived in Kispiox for Waigyet's death feast, the village was dark, the bumpy dirt streets were empty and there were few lights on in any of the houses. At the upriver end of the reserve village, dozens of cars and trucks were parked in the frost-covered mud around the community hall, where the village dogs were roaming around in packs. Groups of children were hurrying to and from their parents' pickup trucks in the cold night air with boxes full of food and goods, and Wii Seeks stood at the door of the community hall, leaning against the wall and smoking a cigarette. He pulled his short-brimmed fedora down over his eyes, but I could see how he was still carrying a lot of sadness with the death of his grandmother, Elsie Morrison, Waigyet. Like he had said that day the Suskwa roadblock went up at the Bulkley River bridge, she was 82 after all, and that was a good age to live to, but it was clear he wasn't quite used to the idea of not having her around.

It was also clear that he was already exhausted. The proceedings had just begun, and it was only 6:30, but he was a principal sponsor of the feast so he had several busy hours to go before he could sit down. There were guests to be seated and contribution records to be kept and goods to be distributed and Wii Seeks hadn't been up to much effort since Waigyet died over at the Hazelton hospital, where Wii Seeks would sit at her bedside and report to her about the roadblocks, and she had knitted socks, toques and sweaters for the people out at Sam Green Creek. Now she was gone, and at least the grieving was almost over. "It helps to lift a lot of my grief," he said, and he tossed his cigarette away, distracted by the commotion inside the hall. "It helps a lot. It will hurt later. She was a warehouse of knowledge."

Wii Seeks brought me inside and looked around for the right place for this guest to sit. He and the other fireweed chiefs had spent the last hour escorting guests to their seats, and already the feast hall was full. Stacks of boxes teetered several feet high on tables. There were boxes of groceries, blankets, clothes and hardware, boxes of bread, boxes of salmon, berries and canned goods. It looked like an IGA store, or a major relief operation after a natural disaster. About 500 people were seated throughout the hall beneath the hoisted basketball hoops, arranged by clan, rank, wilp and village at a series of long tables from the entrance doors to the "Welcome to Kispiox" sign above the stage. Children and babies climbed along the tables or sat at their parents' feet and scrawled their names with crayons on white sheets of paper.

All of this was illegal from 1884 to 1951. During the time of the potlatch and tamanawas laws, Oakalla prison was a routine destination for Indians whose crimes were dancing or giving things away. The point of the law, according to Indian Superintendent I. W. Powell, was the "control of the Indians," and in a 1914 letter to the great Katzie chief Simon Pierre, J. D. McLean made clear the government's purposes: "Sports or amusements which do not interfere with the serious business of obtaining a livelihood are not objected to by the department as long as they are properly conducted." Obtaining a livelihood meant fishing for the canneries, working on the cannery lines or working in the sawmills. That's where Indians were needed, and it did no good to have them roaming about the coast from one potlatch to another, participating in a social and economic system that bolstered the aboriginal political system and undermined the Crown. B.C.'s Indian leaders seemed convinced, however, that the law was simply misguided, as a December 1918 petition of Kwagewlth chiefs to Duncan Campbell Scott, the deputy superintendent of Indian Affairs, makes clear. The chiefs advised Scott: "We feel the government has not been fully and correctly informed about the potlatch and we would respectfully ask you to send a good straight man to come and see all the Indians so that you might know exactly what a potlatch is. We think the law is not right and that you have been mistaken in stopping the Indians from giving away money to our friends. We see our white friends giving presents to one another and why can we not do the same? Our white friends give feasts. Why can we not do the same?" Scott answered the chiefs the following month: "Whatever the purpose or principle of the potlatch may be, the fact remains that potlatches are attended by prolonged idleness and waste of time, by ill-advised and wanton giving away of property and by immorality." Later that year, three Kwagewlth chiefs wrote again to Scott, again trying to enlighten him about the social functions of the potlatch: "We ... request the right to support our poor and sick and those out of work ... we desire that the Indian Act be amended in this respect so as to allow us to take proper care of our poor." The chiefs also suggested that since each Indian was levied a $5 poll tax, and each Indian dog a $1 dog tax, it was only fair that Indians be permitted to vote, too. Scott wrote back that Section 149 of the Indian Act would be upheld, reminding them that the law "forbids the giving away or paying or giving back of money, goods or articles of any sort at any Indian festival, dance or other ceremony." He was silent about the vote.

The potlatch persisted. There were just too many Indian villages scattered throughout B.C. and not enough Indian agents to keep an eye on everybody, and wherever there was a substantial police presence, the feast and the spirit dance went underground. Spies, Mounties, Indian agents, missionaries and fishing company clerks were mustered against it.

The situation was ridiculous. A 1921 report by one RCMP Sergeant Angermann to the notorious Indian agent and justice of the peace William Halliday, contains this intelligence, about the Kwagewlths of Alert Bay: "There were meetings where a certain amount of fruit and refreshments were given away and perhaps some of the fruit carried away from the meetings." Halliday's files also show a letter from the missionary Rev. R. C. Scott, regarding suspicions about the Kwagewlth chief Jack Nacknakim: "I have reason to think that some sort of celebration is being planned in connection with the naming of this child [Nacknakim's newborn daughter]. Jack has been buying a good deal of stuff at the store, towels, ribbon, gum boots, popcorn, etc., etc., but just what he intends to do with it I am not sure. I have not seen the things myself, but have been told by the clerks at the cannery store that he is getting some of these articles enumerated."

The first attempt at enforcing the law ended in failure in August 1889, when Hemasak, a Kwagewlth from Mamalilikula, was tried by a local justice of the peace, convicted and sentenced to six months, and then released after some unnamed non-native "friends" appealed the conviction successfully. Judge Matthew Begbie, known in white folklore as "the hanging judge," found no evidence that Hemasak knew what crime he was pleading guilty to and the judge himself conceded that white people didn't seem to know what a potlatch was, anyway. As the years passed, police and Indian agents in newfangled gas boats sneaked through the channels and up rivers and lingered at the outskirts of villages to see whether there was any evidence of mass gift-giving or dancing. Missionaries encouraged some Christian Indians to petition Victoria for the enforcement of the law. Other Indians, and some white people, petitioned Victoria with requests that the feast system be left alone. The newspapers were full of the controversy, alternating between lurid descriptions of the "heathen" practice and sympathetic accounts comparing the potlatch to European wedding feasts, funerals, cocktail parties and square dances.

It was in Kwagewlth territory that the law was tested, and where it was most rigorously enforced in a period of coastal history the Kwagewlths remember as the "Halliday Terrorism," after Indian agent William Halliday. Although the court records are not complete, it would appear that about 50 men and women, mostly Kwagewlths, were convicted under the potlatch law. At least half of them were given prison sentences of two to six months and sent in shackles to Oakalla prison. Among the spoils obtained by Ottawa and shipped to museums throughout the world were hundreds of works of Kwagewlth art: masks, carvings, rattles, headdresses, beaded blankets, staffs, dance aprons, whistles and drums. Still, the potlatch continued, with lookouts posted on cliffs and downriver neighbours keeping watch from their fishing sites. As a Kwagewlth chief explained to anthropologist Franz Boas in 1896: "It is a strict law that bids us dance. It is a strict law that bids us distribute our property among our friends and neighbours. It is a good law. Let the white man observe his law, we shall observe ours."

So the Gitksans obeyed their law, too, perplexing as it was to outsiders, and it was bad enough just stumbling out of the bush into these lights, but on top of that this was my first death feast and I wasn't sure what to do.

"I'm glad you came," Wii Seeks said, taking my arm. "I'll put you over here."

He sat me with the wolves, which was fortunate for me because at Gitksan feasts you stay seated for the duration, and I knew some of my neighbours at the table. Homer Muldoe was away in Vancouver, so I got his place, beside his brother Arnie Shanoss, Sabamgoss, in the House of Niist, David

Blackwater. Niist presided over his wilp from the end of the long table. There were about 40 wolves at Niist's table, mostly from Kuldoe, that old village still beyond the reach of roads but little more than a graveyard now. At the table across from us sat more wolves, from Kuldoe and Kisgegas, a village also long since abandoned. Parallel to these wolves sat the wolves of Kispiox.

The fireweed chiefs hosting this feast would not sit until the proceedings were over. They would be dead tired by then. They stood at the back of the hall, or at the door, receiving guests, recording contributions, disbursing gifts and keeping records of attendance. The wolves, eagles and frogs were seated in their places, as were members of the corresponding Wet'suwet'en clans, the frog, small frog, wolf, fireweed and beaver.

Sitting next to me, Walter Blackwater, Deeskw, looked at the food in front of him and leaned over to me.

"In the olden days, they didn't have this kind of bread," he said. "They have all kinds of fish and wild animals. That's why they have the mountains and their own territories. There wasn't even an inch open."

So this was Deeskw. I'd heard stories about him. Deeskw had seen a lot of this country, he's well respected in the feast house and I was fortunate to sit with him. A 66-year-old father of five, Deeskw had spoken for more than eight hours one day in the early stages of the land claims trial in Smithers, simply describing his house territory, and spent another seven hours the next day describing a neighbouring house territory. He completed his recital in the Gitksan language because he wanted to make sure he got it right, but also because to speak thoroughly and accurately about this countryside is impossible in English. Deeskw spent his boyhood out on the land with his father, Jimmy Blackwater, who held the exalted name Wii Minosik, and Deeskw was trapping alone by the time he was seventeen. He worked his trapline until he was 25, when he started logging, but a short time later he went to work for the Cassiar Cannery on the coast and kept his cannery job the rest of his working life. But it is this countryside that he knows better than any of the cannery machines that made his hands and arms so strong over the years, and it is the countryside he prefers. A few months earlier on the Mitten main road an RCMP officer found Deeskw cutting up a moose at the side of the road. He told Deeskw he wouldn't charge an old man for not having a licence, but to stay put, hand over his rifle and wait for the game warden. Deeskw said he wouldn't have minded going before a judge on a hunting charge, since to his mind he had a right to hunt for his family, and he never surrendered that right by treaty or otherwise. But the Mountie said he wouldn't charge him, and told him to wait for the game warden. Deeskw waited in the freezing cold for five hours for the game warden. The warden left him the moose's left hind leg and by the night of Waigyet's feast Deeskw was still waiting to get his rifle back from the Mounties.

Deeskw was right about the olden days, when the land was rich and there wasn't an inch open between the chiefs' house territories. There were salmon runs of almost unimaginable abundance, berry grounds and wild fruits and vegetables. There was caribou, goat, groundhog, beaver, deer, lake fish, wolverine, marten and wolf. There was crabapple, rosehip, swamp cranberry, huckleberry, blueberry and saskatoon. There was hazelnut, the riceroot bulb, fireweed honey and soapberry.

The year's fishing — which the Gitksan and Wet'suwet'en considered to be part of an ongoing diplomatic relationship with the allied nations of salmon — began with the spring salmon runs, followed by the sockeye and pink, a break for berry picking in the late summer and then the coho and steelhead. The rivers were alive with industry. The men were busy at their dipnetting stations, gaffing rocks and salmon weirs — elaborate structures operated under carefully regulated regimes governed by the needs of upriver villages and spawning escapement. The women worked in the smokehouses, cutting, stripping and curing fish in specialized processing operations that produced 24 different salmon delicacies.

There were small-scale streamclearing operations to be undertaken, hillsides to be burned in the early spring to prepare the ground for berry fields, bug-infested groves of trees to be selectively burned before the larvae hatched, piles of pink salmon to be left for the bears in case they turned hungry and dangerous in the coming winter. The land provided medicines such as cow parsnip, Indian hellebore and devil's club and yellow pond lily, each harvested at the appropriate time of the year for the appropriate purpose. They cured ulcers, healed wounds, treated cuts and skin ailments, and controlled headaches. Elaborate laws governed the hunting and trapping round, laws that ranged from rules about the maintenance of trail cairns to the size of marmot snares to ensure against trapping yearlings, and the laws were reinforced in the feast house with every birth and every death.

The talk at the table was about the roadblock, and what the government was going to do, and how things were going in the blockade camp, how old Haa'txw was holding out, and whether it was getting really cold at night, or just cold. Deeskw made a point of saying how pleased he was that the chiefs with territories in the Suskwa were taking a stand.

The fireweeds were making the rounds with bowls of fish soup, and somewhere in the hall Willie Morrison was speaking into a microphone, announcing contributions and calling out the names of donors. The wolves at this table had already reckoned that things looked certain that the tally was going to exceed Mabel White's feast tally last week, which drew $18,000 in cash.

Deeskw peered over his spectacles. They were held together with a rubber band keeping the bridge together, some thread to hold the right armpiece attached and tape to keep it behind his ear. He leaned forward so I could hear him over the chatter.

"It may be too late," he said, and at first I wasn't sure what he meant. "Some places, the land is cleared right off. All the trees are gone, and you can't put traps in the snow. At least we're starting to stop things, because they're getting in there way further off now. It would be nice if we could have done this years ago. Years ago."

It was hard to hear him over the commotion around us, the fireweeds walking with trays of food for the tables, Willie Morrison calling out the rolls and the gentle chatter of old friends at a funeral. As the fireweeds continued their rounds, disbursing gifts and talking to mourners, Morrison's rollcall continued.

"Wii Seeks, $2,000. Mas Gak, $100. Don Morrison, $500. $1,500, Beverley Anderson. $1,500, Pete Muldoe. $1,500, Danny Gagnon. Chris Gagnon, $40. Lorraine Mitchell, $100."

Some old women were busy knitting. Others were furiously jotting notes on sheets of foolscap paper, recording the names of contributors, cancelling past debts and noting future obligations. As Deeskw spoke, the apples, bread, fruit and boxes of cookies piled higher and higher on our table and on the tables around us.

"Vincent Muldoe, $100," Morrison called out. "Graham McPherson, $20. Marvin Turner, $25 and enough food for a year. Thank you. $50, Chester McPherson. Thank you. $100,

Charlie. Charlie Muldoe. $150, Elaine Muldoe. Brian Muldoe, $100. Joe Wilson, $100. Thank you."

Morrison continued to call. The names were from all over the Gitksan and Wet'suwet'en territories, and from Vancouver and Prince Rupert and Prince George and Terrace. At a table in the corner the old ladies continued their hurried knitting, and one of them was adding up the totals on a calculator. A young man with a perplexed look added with his fingers.

"Sampson Muldoe, $20. Haircut," Morrison called out. The word "haircut" appeared from time to time, denoting the relative of a fireweed contributing to the feast. All I could gather about the word haircut was that in the old days a custom was that mourners would burn their hair to show their grief over a lost relative or their sympathy for the bereaved.

All the while, a small grey-haired woman in glasses, Helena Joseph, stood to Morrison's left, silent, head bowed, a button blanket wrapped around her frail shoulders. Helena Joseph was taking the name Waigyet, inheriting it from Elsie, and inheriting the rank, territories and privileges that go along with it. Helena's husband was Gisday Wa, the Wet'suwet'en leader Alfred Joseph, and with this high name in their family it would be a particularly powerful family now.

Each of the contributors attested to the ascendancy's legitimacy, and by their presence and their acceptance of gifts, the mourners acknowledged Helena Joseph's right to be known thereafter as Waigyet.

Art Wilson, Wii Muugalsxw, waved to me from across the hall and came over to chat. Wii Muugalsxw, a ranking Kispiox wolf, smiled, shook my hand and after a while he pointed to the roll of bills in his left hand. "I better go and support my dad, and put some money in for my kids," he said. His children are from his first wife, a white woman, so the kids were adopted by the fireweeds. The fact that they are fireweeds apparently made him a haircut. Things were becoming clearer.

This is what the anthropologists describe as an economic system based on balanced reciprocity in which perishable wealth is converted into non-perishable status and kinship-based economic units engage in social, economic and co-operative relations among themselves. For the Gitksan and Wet'suwet'en, the feast house is the credit union, the House of Commons, the land titles office and the community centre. Disputes are arbitrated, debts are settled, friendships renewed and community stability is reinforced. Each feast is a minor economic engine that disburses goods throughout society, and each transaction is recorded and acknowledged.

There wasn't much effort made at stamping out the feast system in Gitksan country. The hapless Captain Fitzstubbs, who had visited Kispiox in 1888 to find no Indian willing to acknowledge his salutation, visited Gitwangak that same year to tell them to desist in their potlatches. The Anglican missionary who had urged him on, one H. K. Pocock, recalled in a letter how the Indians had laughed and called the law a "weak baby." Pocock later remarked to Fitzstubbs: "For over two hours I expected an attack, but your courage and good humour surprised and awed the people ... I was told afterwards that most of those who were present thought you would be killed."

In 1889, Fitzstubbs conceded that his exhortations in Gitwangak had been a "blunder," and he suggested that perhaps the feast wasn't such a bad institution anyway, since it functioned as a market, provided a public forum for tribal affairs, served as something of a "benefit society" and besides, any attempt to enforce the anti-potlatch law would be regarded as fiercely annoying and may produce among the natives "a disinclination to obey the law on other points."

The missionaries still disliked it, but by 1897 the local Indian agent, R.E. Loring, reckoned that the Gitksan feast system would soon exist "only in memory."

By 11:10 p.m., five hours after the feast began, the total raised in Waigyet's honor was $25,880, and the fireweed house chiefs began the disbursements. Eric McPherson, the fireweed Luu Goom'kw, started his long walk from table to table with a list of names, and socks and scarves for everyone who participated at the Sam Green roadblocks at the Babine. The Hazelton hospital ended up with the colour television set Earl Muldoe, Elsie's nephew, bought for her during her stay there. He decided to donate it to the hospital in appreciation. There were gravediggers to be paid, costs borne by relatives and friends who assisted in the feast, various debts to be settled, transportation costs subsidized, acts of charity rewarded and some needy people to attend to who just didn't have much food or money. One of the fireweeds carried a new rifle to someone, but I couldn't make out who it was. Marvin Sampson got a new barbeque set in a box, and at his table were sweaters, blankets and a box of food. A lot of the younger men deliver fish from their nets in the Skeena River to the old people in the villages during the salmon runs. Sampson is one of those young men.

By 12:45 p.m., $7,000 of the money collected had been disbursed and Alvin Weget was at the microphone, calling out the names of the people who helped with the feast and the amounts they would receive. They were people who moved the coffin from place to place, or transported relatives in their cars and pickup trucks.

"When I come to feasts I look at this and I say, 'Wow, look at this.' There's no animosity," said Sabamgoss, who was sitting at my left. "Glen Vowell sitting with Kispiox and

Gitanmaax sitting with Gitsegukla. I think, why doesn't it work outside? It doesn't."

Sabamgoss is the disc jockey and commentator for Radio Free Gitanmaax, the pirate radio station the chiefs established as part of their campaign to assert authority in their territories. The government-owned Insurance Corporation of B.C. still sends them safe-driving ads to play, even though the station is "illegal," and Sabamgoss plays them. The warning letters from the Canadian Radio-television and Telecommunications Commission Sabamgoss tosses in the garbage.

By this time, Alvin Weget, Pete Muldoe and Lloyd Morrison were walking the aisles between tables with Helena Joseph. Alvin was picking $10 and $20 bills from a silver washbasin and passing them to Helena, who in turn handed them to the seated witnesses. They were headed slowly towards the wolves and I wasn't sure what to do. I'm seated at Homer Muldoe's place in the feast house. He wasn't here because he was in court in Vancouver fighting some traffic case. Do I step back?

"No, that would show disrespect," Sabamgoss said.

But this isn't my place.

"Maybe you should take your brother's money," I suggested.

"You're sitting there," he said. Earlier, I took an apple put in Homer's place. The soup and the salmon and the rice and the potatoes and the cake were for me, but the apple was technically one of Homer's apples.

"Well, you took something of his," said a wolf in a Kispiox baseball cap sitting on the far side of the table. "In the old days, you'd have to put up a feast for doing that."

He's serious.

"Don't worry about it," he adds.

Then Antiigililbix, the 80-year-old Mary Johnson, took

the microphone and began to speak slowly in the old language. She spoke quietly, and everyone listened carefully.
"Waigyet," I heard her say every once in a while, among all
the other words I didn't understand. Each chief was asked to
call back the name Waigyet in turn, acknowledging the
ascendancy.

Antiigililbix continued her address and Alvin and Lloyd
continued their rounds. It had taken them an hour to get
through the hall, and now they were getting closer to the
wolves, and Sabamgoss tips me to sit in the vacant chair to
his immediate right. No problem. Arnie and Lloyd arrived
with the cash-filled silver washbasin, and the young girl sitting across from me got $10. Sabamgoss got $75. Deeskw got
$75. Homer got $40, even though he wasn't there. I got $20.

After two hours, Antiigililbix was still speaking into the
microphone in the old language and Alvin and Lloyd were
still making their rounds.

I noticed that some new names were appearing in the
liturgy, and I noticed too that Beverley Anderson, Yok, was
standing beside Willie Morrison, who had followed
Antiigililbix. Beverley was becoming Maht, one of Waigyet's
names, and Vernon Joseph took the name Daakhluumgyet.

It was good to see Beverley's long service acknowledged
this way. I knew her as a community health nurse, a blockade
advocate and a source of amazing huckleberry jam, and after
a half-hour standing beside Morrison she came to visit our
table. She was obviously fatigued, and she leaned up against
the wall behind me.

"I'm not supposed to sit down," she said. She had only
found out that day that the name Maht was to be passed to
her. She was still beneath Gitluudahl in the wilp, but she had
her own strong ideas about what advice to give him, and she
talked about her plans.

"Everything on a territory can support a house," she said.

"For me, first of all, I want to heal the family. I want to get the family together. I'd like to make it a sanctuary. If a family does it, you'll see other families doing it. Look around here tonight," she said, leaning her head back against the wall. "A lot of people, good people, are in ill health. They're not well. And they're depressed. But look at my uncle." She indicates Gitluudahl. "He's over 80. He goes trapping, hunting, fishing, gathering remedies, and he looks after the territory."

The speeches began. Gitluudahl, Wii Seeks, and then Delgamuukw, Kenny Muldoe, the named plaintiff in the Gitksans' massive land claims case against the Crown.

"Ladies and gentlemen," Delgamuukw said, "we are very pleased by what you have shown us here tonight. The strength and the wisdom you have shown us. We have seen the transfer of a number of names, and I am happy to see the respect that you have shown to my late aunt. I thank you all. And God bless you all."

And then Dora Wilson-Kenni: "I wish to thank you, thank you for the gifts you have given us tonight, and to allow us to be a witness to the work you have done tonight on behalf of a very great lady. Elsie would have been very proud of you. She showed only respect and love for me and my family and this we will never forget."

Then another chief spoke briefly, then another, and another. It was 3:30 a.m. when everything wrapped up.

Shaking hands with the people as they left, Wii Seeks said he felt a lot better.

"There must be a God up there," he said, and he pushed back the brim of his short-brimmed fedora and smiled. "And I'm sure he only wants the best for Wii Seeks."

It had been a long time in the planning and the waiting, and now that Elsie's feast was done, the chiefs would be back to their plans for a new roadblock, this time in the Kispiox Valley. The plan was to shut off one of the key conduits of timber traffic in B.C.'s sprawling northwest country, through which Westar Timber was taking 500,000 cubic metres of timber each year, the bulk of its entire annual consumption.

Deeskw gathered his things together, and I put my apples and oranges and bread in a bag, and headed out for the long drive through the dark to the Suskwa bushcamp.

"Good thing, that Suskwa roadblock," Deeskw said. His back was stiff and he pulled himself slowly from his chair. "It's got to be all of B.C. To shut down all of it. Everything. Then you'll see something going on. It's not far, not far. Pretty soon, Westar will be all over this country, and the same is happening everywhere else.

"That's why I want to see the whole of B.C. roadblocked."

S I X

BEHIND
ENEMY LINES

A few days after Waigyet's feast, sitting at Thomas Atrill's kitchen table with one of Atrill's ten cats on my lap and one of Atrill's seven dogs barking outside, I was reminded about something else Deeskw had said, when I was sitting with the wolves in the Kispiox hall. It was about Dimlahamid.

"There was a war. A group of people were hiding in the mountains, and people left it because there was a war. They had good reason to leave. So they went. They spread all over. To Kuldoe, to Kisgegas, everywhere."

And he had said: "But it was a good place, I guess. Like a city. A big city."

If it was a war these Indians wanted it was a war they would get and you could take that to the bank, if Thomas Atrill had anything to do with it. Atrill had heard just about enough about these roadblocks. He was sick to the teeth of Indians stopping him in his red Datsun pickup at that blockade on the Suskwa Main road on his way back home and as far as he was concerned the whole thing had gone on long enough. If something wasn't done soon, the Indians would have the run of the whole countryside and a white man would have as much rights as a fish on dry land.

That's what he'd told the lawyer from the attorney-general's department down at the Hazelton RCMP substation. "Mackenzie's his name," Atrill said, showing me the lawyer's business card. "James Mackenzie."

Mackenzie had been skulking around the Hazelton area for a couple of days, gathering evidence against the Indians for the B.C. attorney-general's department, preparing affidavits and putting marks on maps so that when the police were called in against the Gitksan, they'd know where to go and who to arrest, and the forest companies would have all the sworn statements they'd need when it came time to file their writs of summons in B.C. Supreme Court.

The RCMP had called Atrill on the telephone and asked him to come down and talk to the government man about the Indians and that's what Atrill did, because Atrill intended to do his part, and that's what he'd told Mackenzie. For now, waiting for the big moment, his part meant playing a sort of wartime civil-defence role from his second-hand store in the Bulkley Valley bottomlands behind the Suskwa roadblock. Behind enemy lines, after a manner of speaking.

Task One: Send a Petition to the Prime Minister.

"Here it is," he said, pushing the petition across from his side of his kitchen table. "I've got about 100 signatures by now."

We, the undersigned, demand that the Government of Canada take the following steps as soon as possible: (1) To uphold the laws of this country regarding our property rights, our use of public roads, our right to carry on enterprises such as logging, fishing, hunting and any other legal pursuit. Also, the right to own land without undue restriction, such as "lis pendens" or aboriginal land claims. This must include the right to freedom from harassment, as well. And (2), we demand that the Government of Canada do all that is necessary to bring about a just settlement of all claims, valid or otherwise, initiated by aboriginal persons and groups against the non-Indian people of Canada.

The Indians should have been put in their place long ago, Atrill said, adding that he wasn't afraid to say it. He sat there in his kitchen amidst an indescribable clutter of gimcracks and bric-a-brac, a telephone in the design of a tiny piano, an odd, physics-lab steel ball clock, an aquarium filled with tropical fish, and ballet-dancer dolls and hundreds of mugs tucked into every nook and cranny. I looked hard, but I couldn't find a square foot of uncluttered space in his kitchen or his living room. I sat and listened.

The plump, red-cheeked 62-year-old Atrill sat there with his neatly clipped grey hair and his trim military moustache and discussed the state of affairs that led him to enter the fray.

For starters, he grew up about five miles from here on his father's farm, one of twelve children in the family. He was born in the Hazelton hospital, served as a railroad conductor with the Canadian National Railway, spent 33 years with the CNR, worked as a steam engineer and a carpenter and helped haul the beams for the very bridge the Suskwa chiefs were blockading even as we spoke.

"There are rumblings," Atrill said, to make the point that he was not alone in his views. "People have to work for a living, and they're not able to go to work, and sooner or later these Indians are not going to be able to stop them. Things are going to get really bad, and somebody's going to get killed."

And it was high time the authorities started playing for keeps, by his way of thinking.

"If you jump in there and you have more guns, then you

win. What we need to do, and we should have done it 30 years ago, and that's march in the army if they don't stop kicking about it. I think it's high time the government march the troops in there and tell them this is Canada. We cannot put up with this kind of extortion and blackmail. These people are bandits and they are breaking the law. So, you send an emissary to all the reserves and tell them that this is Canada, whether they like it or not. And of course, they will disagree. And they should have marched in the militia and raised the flag and said, 'This is Canada whether you like it or not.' And it's still not too late to do that.

"But I don't like anybody to suggest that I'm a radical or anything like that."

And to Atrill's credit there was nothing particularly radical in what he was saying, since his views quite accurately reflected a substantial body of opinion among the white people in the Gitksan and Wet'suwet'en territories, and despite Atrill's relative isolation in these cottonwood groves and hayfields deep in the bush country west of Smithers, his view of the land claims controversy reflected with a remarkable degree of precision the provincial government's stance on the subject, which is that there is no such thing as a legitimate Indian land claim, Indians have land rights only to their reserves, and Indians didn't even own the land before the whites arrived because they didn't understand what it meant to own land.

The only difference between Atrill and the Queen in the Delgamuukw trial is that Atrill's language is more concise: "These bastards" is what he calls the plaintiffs' lawyers. "I would like to make it clear," Atrill went on, sitting upright in his chair, "that never, at no time, did Indians have any legitimate claims to the land except what had been allotted to them." As for the notion of a sophisticated, land-holding society with roots in these mountains going back thousands of years, Atrill's view is this: "Their morals were no better than barnyard animals and [the missionaries] had to constantly remind them that civilized people always wore clothes."

And if anybody needed any further proof of the Indians' continuing backwardness, Atrill offered this, over a second cup of coffee: "Indians are about 99 per cent NDP. I don't know why an Indian's got to be so dumb that he's got to be an NDPer. Ignorance brings on the belief in socialism."

No, he simply wouldn't have any more of this carry-on. It wasn't that he didn't like Indians. After all, his wife of four years was an Indian, and as we spoke, Carol poured the coffee and put out cookies and every now and then said "you can say that again" or confirmed her husband's points with "I think it's wrong, too." A Cree who grew up in a convent in Grouard, Alberta, Carol is an area homemaker who cooks meals for shut-ins for the social services ministry. What she has to say about these Gitksans is, "If they want to go back to their old ways, they'd starve to death," and about Tom she says, "I've learned a lot from him."

Atrill learned about Indians by growing up among them. Not that he mixed with Indians, but he knew a thing or two, and one thing was that all this land claims talk was inspired by money-hungry lawyers and it was a new thing. There was no history to it.

"All my life I got along with Indians and there was no talk about land claims," he said. "It's a recent development."

To be fair, Atrill wasn't alive on April 20, 1915, when Mool'xan told the McKenna-McBride commissioners in Gitsegukla, "This land belongs to our forefathers that have died" and not to the B.C. government, and Atrill wasn't with me in Gitsegukla more than 70 years later, when old David Milton stood in his weaselskin-tassled button blanket on the front porch of his house with his fourteen grandchildren, and said, "It has been years and years and years and the government still does not grant us our land claim." On April 21, 1915, in Gitanmaax, Chief Spookw told the commissioners, "We were asking from the government to give us our land back ... to get rid of the Indian Act for us. This is what we have been asking the government for the last seven years." And Atrill wasn't there in Gitanmaax that day in 1986 when Ralph Michell, only a few weeks after he had inherited the name Wii Seeks, explained: "As our forefathers did, we will continue to have our feasts and we will continue to fight for what is ours." And Atrill wasn't in Gitwangak in 1915 when Chief Jim said, bluntly, "We don't ask no money from any man. All we are asking is to get our own land back. I got a tongue and I don't want to be talking different stories every minute ... I told you before I want to get all the land back from the government." And Atrill wasn't there 70 years later in Gitwangak when Gwiis Gyen told me, "I know the names we have given all of the land, and I know who owns it."

I couldn't see how it could be called a "recent development." Atrill shrugged, and answered, "What happened then has no bearing whatsoever on what's happening now."

It was a few years before the Atrills moved out from Neepawa, Ontario, that the returning Canadian Boer War veterans were given "land scrip" among their benefits and some of that property included Wet'suwet'en ranches in the Bulkley Valley. The Indians' houses were burned down and they were driven off to make way for the settlers. And it was also true that Atrill was born in 1927, the year the federal government passed amendments to the Indian Act that made it virtually illegal to raise the question of aboriginal title until the Act was again amended in 1951.

Still, he had grown up here, almost precisely in the middle of the 22,000 square miles of the Gitksan and Wet'suwet'en chiefs' wilp territories. So I didn't see how this was coming as something of a surprise.

"You see," Atrill said, "the relationship was quite different when I was growing up. The Indians were on their reserves, and they didn't interfere with the whites, and we were just like in two worlds. We were neighbourly, though.

"But my dad never gave in to them," he was quick to point out. "They would come by our place in their wagons and they didn't know how to control their children. They still can't control their children. Well, my dad took out his rifle and killed two of their dogs. They were going after our animals. The Indians were going to have an uprising, but my dad never gave an inch."

And then there was the time that an Indian was crossing their farm to go fishing, and Atrill's mother told him to go around the ranch, not across it, and as Atrill remembers, "he was really threatening about it. We were just little kids, but we would have killed him, I think. But he went around, anyway."

Things were different then. He was right about that.

I remembered old Jeff Harris, Luus, telling stories about how the white kids in Hazelton didn't play with the Indian kids. The Indians weren't allowed in at the dances at the Hazelton hall until the time after the war when Luus was playing in the dance band and the Indian veterans showed up, and there was a near riot when they weren't allowed in. It started when a white man spat in an Indian veteran's face. But Harris and his dance band refused to play any more music until the Indian boys were allowed in, so the doors were opened, and the Indians and the whites danced together. In Old Town, as Hazelton's called, things started to change after that. But change comes slowly.

"If Indians didn't go to dances it's because they didn't like to do that sort of thing," Atrill said. "And sure, businessmen used to advertise that they had 'all-white help,' or signs that said 'no Indians here,' but I don't think it bothered the Indians that much because they liked to stick to themselves anyway."

These days, with all the talk about the land claim and the roadblocks closing off the forests to Westar, there was a definite mood of uncertainty in the countryside, and it was tough on a lot of the non-Indians, despite the fact that the chiefs repeatedly reminded them that they were welcome in the territories and even if they got everything they were after in *Delgamuukw versus The Queen*, they weren't after white people's homes, their farms or their ranches.

It was tough on people like Helen Campbell. It had been 60 years since Helen and her husband Ted rumbled over a bumpy dirt track into the Kispiox Valley in a 1925 Hudson with their three children and all their worldly belongings, including a goat suspended from a makeshift pen lashed to one of the Hudson's running boards. Still, when the 78-year-old secretary of the Kispiox Valley Farmers' Institute sat at the kitchen table of her ranch house and looked out into the rain over the brown grass meadow, she was unconvinced. Her ranch was private property, so why was she confronted on the main street of Hazelton, and she an older lady walking with a cane, to be told her ranch was on some chief's property? That's what she said she wanted to know, and she wanted the outside world to know that some white people were plainly nervous about all this talk about the "land claim" and the "court case" and Indian ownership and Indian jurisdiction.

Everything seemed so simple in the old days, she said, even when the wolves chased their cattle right up to the house or the time around Christmas in 1944 when the house burned down and the family lived with the animals in the barn until spring and it used to take five hours to get to Hazelton with a team of horses and a sleigh. Everybody seemed to get along just fine.

"Now, it's not so simple," she said. "It's yes and no ... One man told me it don't pay to speak out. There's always somebody who takes things into their own hands and if you find a beef shot and lying in the woods, you can't prove anything in a court of law, can you?" Not that any rancher has found a beef shot and lying in the woods, and not that she regrets leaving the Dakota territory all those years ago looking for open country where the game hadn't been all killed off, but still, it's not like all the white people are just going to pack it in and move off somewhere else.

Then there's Marty Allen, a 79-year-old rancher who seemed even more confused than old Helen. He takes a hard line and he's not afraid to speak out. He says: "I own my property and God help the Indian who comes along to take it away from me." And he says: "If they win, we would have to have a little roar here, just like in South Africa. And there's more whites than there is Indians." But in almost the same breath he says the Indians are right when they talk about what's been going on in the forest industry, and how Indian communities have suffered the most, and how the provincial government should no longer abdicate its responsibilities to deal fair and square with the Gitksan and Wet'suwet'en. And he says the Indians deserve, at the very least, a hefty financial settlement for what's been lost.

If not for his remarks about the forest industry Allen's views might come close to the stance taken by most people in New Hazelton, where Pete Weeber, who was the mayor when I talked to him about things, was also the woodlands manager for Westar Timber. The 49-year-old Weeber and his wife Linda raised seven children in the 21 years they've lived in the area and they had tied their fortunes, like so many of New Hazelton's 1,000 residents, to The Company. The Company began as Columbia Cellulose, evolved into Canadian Cellulose, and somewhere along the line the local operations became B.C. Timber, which became part of the New Democratic Party's 1972-75 acquisition of assets under the B.C. Resources Investment Corporation, of which the returning Social Credit government divested itself with an uproarious scheme to sell it back to British Columbians, and when the dust settled the original Columbia Cellulose tree farm licences were the scenes of some of the worst forest practices in Canadian history and The Company became Westar Timber.

Said Weeber: "This court case puts the whole countryside on the line. It's pretty hard to imagine. It's this signing away of the whole countryside that we fear. It's the established order of things, property rights, your right to make a living."

Besides, he said, the Indians couldn't pull it off.

"We have tried to do business with the native people and it doesn't work. It's hard to imagine these people running the whole country, that's all."

That's the thing about New Town, as it's known. It's tried to do business and it's boomed and built and settled down with the forest industry over the past half-century, first with the railroad and then when the Yellowhead Highway pushed through, and it straddles the highway with a cafe, a store, another cafe, a gas station, another store, a bar, a delicatessen, a motel and another store, and perhaps there are a few things the town can't imagine.

But if Weeber can't imagine the Indians running the whole country, he discovered to his own rude surprise on an autumn day in 1988 that they can certainly run a roadblock. Wii Seeks taught Weeber about that on the morning of September 28, soon after Weeber, road contractor Dave Hamblin and bridge contractors Peter Thwaites and Dean Welsh arrived at the outskirts of the Babine bush camp at Sam Green Creek.

They were met by Wii Seeks and Eric McPherson, Luu Goom'kw. Weeber told them that he and the contractors were there to start work on the abutments to the bridge the Gitksan chiefs had vowed would never be built.

Weeber and his crew walked over to the head of the road they were pushing to the riverbank and found a centre line pin missing and surveyor's batter boards broken. Weeber was walking towards a rocky outcropping on high ground to radio in for a helicopter to ferry the surveyors across the river when Wii Seeks walked up to him and told him: "This is as far as you go."

Weeber turned and walked away. He headed up a sidehill, followed by the Wet'suwet'en leaders Herb and Marvin George, Herb in his Ford pickup and Marvin in his Toyota pickup. The George brothers let him make his call and turned down the hill, pulling up beside Sabamgoss, of Radio Free Gitanmaax, in his Jeep Cherokee. By the time Weeber got back down the hill he noticed two Indians digging post holes in the middle of the road allowance at the point Wii Seeks had told him he would proceed no further. As the Indians nailed a log on top of the posts, Weeber walked over to Wii Seeks, but Wii Seeks refused to talk to him as long as there was that Westar crewman filming everything with his video camera. By Weeber's recollection, Wii Seeks suggested they walk up the hill, where the following conversation took place.

Weeber: "You are putting up a barricade. Is that meant to stop us?"

Wii Seeks: "We do not want the bridge built."

Weeber said Westar Timber needed the bridge to get access to the timber in the virgin territories north of the

Babine, and Wii Seeks replied: "We don't care about Westar anymore. We're going to personally hold you responsible if any construction takes place here. We know you. We know where you live. We know where to get you. We also know the other guys. We know their names. We know where to find them."

Wii Seeks asked if Weeber intended to continue living in the area, and Weeber responded that he did, he liked the place and he intended to live in the area a long time.

Wii Seeks responded: "Well, you better learn to get along with us."

Weeber swore an affidavit in which he described Wii Seeks' remarks as threatening, and since New Town is a small town he would be concerned for his safety and the safety of his family and his property. Weeber said it didn't put his mind to rest much when Wii Seeks later told Thwaites much the same sort of thing, warning him that the Indians would tear down any bridge the company managed to build and they couldn't count on the police to protect them out there round the clock. And it didn't make him feel any better when Wii Seeks told Westar worker Ross Harris that whether or not the chiefs won in *Delgamuukw versus The Queen* they intended to win whatever the means, to "settle things in their own way," as Harris recalled.

The upshot of it all was that the Westar crew and the Formula Contractors bridgebuilding crew and the Hamblin Industries roadbuilding crew retreated in fairly quick time and as it turned out, the B.C. Court of Appeal stopped the bridge for the duration of *Delgamuukw versus The Queen* in the ruling the dissenting judge warned would "interrupt the established administrative and legal system" west of the Rocky Mountains.

So there was no love lost between New Town's Weeber and the Gitksans.

Then there's Old Town. It's the old Hudson's Bay Company post, the head of sternwheeler navigation on the Skeena, site of the famous 'Ksan museum and art gallery and art school. On a flat bend in the Skeena just shy of its confluence with the Bulkley, there's the Inlander Hotel and the frontier-town falsefront shops, the Hudson's Bay store, the tribal council office over on Omineca Street and the police station. On a bluff overlooking the town is Gitanmaax, and the two neighbouring communities go to school and sometimes work together. Added together, they about match New Town's 1,000 people, but if it's a sphere of influence we're talking about Old Town could add to its team the nearby village of Hagwilget and the mixed Indian-white subdivisions around Two Mile, but all New Town could muster would be South Town, with its bar and its store and its cul-de-sacs and house trailers, and maybe Carnaby a few miles downriver, but there's nothing much there but the mill.

Old Town's mayor, Alice Maitland, doesn't get bothered by the land claim the way New Town's Weeber does. Maitland grew up in the area, raised four children with her tractor-driving husband Bill, and pulls in an income from her gas station in town. She turned 54 when *Delgamuukw versus The Queen* opened in Vancouver and she hasn't much thought about leaving for any reason. She's got a great-grandfather and a grandfather, both white men, buried in the Gitanmaax cemetery, and she has never quite figured out what gives with people like Atrill.

"There are a lot of unanswered questions, but I like the idea of self-government, as long as we get a say in what's happening. We don't have that right now. The forest companies come in and cut the trees and leave. What's interesting about the land claim is that it's an excellent chance for something new to happen."

Then there are people like Ian Anderson. He's a 49-year-old white man, and for ten years he's been Beverley Anderson's husband. Beverley Anderson, Yok, was given one of Waigyet's names, Maht, at the Kispiox feast, and throughout the years Ian has supported the feast system, contributed to the feast system and been rewarded by the feast system. He's an adopted commoner among the wolf clan and he doesn't have a problem with the idea of acknowledging the indigenous authority. "You can get involved," he said. "White people can get involved at just about any level they want. People know where I'm coming from, particularly the elders. You're never turned away. You can always get involved. Everything is open, that's the thing about it ... Anybody can get up and speak."

There were dozens more like Anderson, in one way or another, in and around Gitanmaax and Old Town.

In and around British Columbia, while I sat with Atrill at his second-hand store behind enemy lines, a high-powered political strategist by the name of Patrick Kinsella was busy trying to figure out what British Columbians thought about all this land claims business. While Indian Affairs Minister Pierre Cadieux was waiting to hear the news from his regional headquarters in Vancouver about the latest Gitksan roadblock, Kinsella's Marktrend Marketing Research Inc. delivered a long-awaited opinion survey to Cadieux's office, and the results would have upset Atrill, or maybe just confirmed his worst fears about the "communist-infiltrated and communist-influenced" big city media. The poll showed that an overwhelming majority of British Columbians were about as unaware of the "Indian" point of view as Atrill, but the overwhelming majority believed nevertheless that Indians had legitimate claims to the land. The respondents said land claims should be justly settled, and most white people were inclined to believe what the Indians said about aboriginal title, not what B.C. Premier Bill Vander Zalm or B.C. Indian Affairs Minister Jack Weisgerber or Thomas Atrill or Pete Weeber had to say about the subject.

"Close to 80 per cent believe Indians have legitimate claims which should be settled ... Those opposing settlement are more likely to be of 'just Canadian' ethnic origin, older and higher income than B.C. residents in general," the poll concluded.

The survey also found that British Columbians support land claims settlements even though the majority of British Columbians were, like Weeber and Helen Campbell, of the mistaken view that land claims included private property.

"Both the federal government, and even more so, the provincial government, receive poor ratings for their performance to date on land claims," Marktrend found.

Across the country, a Decima Research poll conducted around the time *Delgamuukw versus The Queen* opened in Vancouver found that most Canadians were so uninformed about aboriginal people that almost one-third of Canadians "failed to indicate even an approximate understanding of the term [aboriginal]." The survey was conducted by University of Calgary sociology professor Rick Ponting with Decima Research, and published by Statistics Canada. If the army was sent in to put down Indian roadblocks, as Atrill thought should be done, the poll results suggest Atrill and his militiamen might get a little bit of a surprise. If he can be defined as among the "very antagonistic" point of view, Atrill shares his antagonism with only two per cent of Canadians, the poll concluded.

As we said our goodbyes that October morning, Atrill had one last point he wanted to make.

"This is Canada," he said. "It's not Indian country."

SEVEN

WHEN GOATS FEASTED MEN

I have heard from the Ancient of Sea that in the east there is a fair land encircled on all sides by blue mountains ... I think that this land will undoubtedly be suitable for the extension of the heavenly task, so that its glory should fill the universe. It is, doubtless, the centre of the world.

The Japanese Emperor Jimmu (712 AD)

Later that night, only a few miles through the bush from Atrill's place, Soup, Josh, 'Noola and Haa'txw sat close to the campfire and poured each other cups of coffee after a dinner of grouse soup, bread and apples. This place was a good choice for a bush camp. Sheltered by the trees from the wind that followed the Bulkley River below the ridge, it was only a short walk through the woods to the roadblock and it allowed a clear view through the trees of any headlights on the road leading off the Yellowhead Highway from the far side of the river.

It was a cold and rainy night. The third train of the

evening passed through the mountains to the south on its
way to Prince Rupert.

"I don't know what's going to happen with the land
claim," Soup said. "Maybe it'll do us good when it's settled.
Those Eskimos up north? They got everything. They got
their own television station, everything. I don't know. The
only thing I want is to have our own mill, so everybody
could work. The Indians will have work. They'll own their
own outfits."

He turned to Josh. "We could have our own out at
Kisgegas, eh?"

Josh smiled. "Yeah. Our own."

Both of them had worked with Wii Seeks and the others
at the Babine blockade over the summer.

"No money in it," Soup said, "but the way I think about
it is that our trapline is more important. So we stopped them
from building the bridge across."

'Noola had been quiet since suppertime. He was busy
with the dishes, and after he'd tidied up he sat and stared into
the fire.

"I think maybe this area, a hundred years from now, will
be the only place left with any forests," he said. "If I had my
way I'd go back 50 years and just log by horses. We were poor
then but we're poor now. Who wants to get rich overnight?"

Soup and Haa'txw stood up from the fire, walked around
behind the kitchen camp shelves and came back with two
willow poles. They took turns poking at the drooping sections of the tarpaulin roof where the rainwater was gathering
in heavy pools.

'Noola went on.

"These people went out hunting, eh? Young men. They
killed a goat, and that was when goats roamed the forest the
way moose do now," he said. "They weren't all up in the
mountains then. These young men, after they killed a goat,

they would laugh. They didn't have any respect for what they were doing. They would take the head and dance around the fire with it. They'd take the hooves and throw them and stick them against the tree. But one young man, he felt sorry for the 'Waak, the young goat. The baby. He'd paint them, and he'd say to them — in the old days, the people would talk to animals — and he said, 'I'll spare you. The next time I see you I won't kill you.' So he marked the forehead with red paint."

Soup and Josh sat back down.

"Then these people got older, and one time they had visitors from outside the area, in Dimlahamid," 'Noola said. "They came to the village, to Dimlahamid, to invite the people to a feast they were going to have. They stayed outside the village. 'Don't bother those people, they want to stay outside Dimlahamid,' is what the older people said. They invited them to a meal, to eat, and they didn't eat. They just sat there.

"There were kids playing and their parents told them not to play where those men were camping. This kid threw a ball, and it went into the bushes, and he looked where the men were camping, and they were laying around in the grass, eating the grass."

This is how it begins, the story of the Stegyawden massacre, one of the central sagas of the Gitksans' great city on the Skeena. It is a story about when goats feasted men, and the great one-horned goat punishes the people of Dimlahamid for showing disrespect to the animals. The dirge the survivor sings as he sees his people slaughtered at the base of the mountain is a song that remains among the possessions of the wilp within which 'Noola now sits, which is the House of Xsimwits'iin.

And so Tom Atrill can say this is Canada, but it is also Indian country, and it is Gitksan country, and Dimlahamid is here, somewhere, and Atrill can't be faulted for not finding it. The RCMP will find the Suskwa roadblock and the bush camp, if it comes to that. Maybe there will be columns of them in riot gear, the way they showed up in New Town that morning when the first Kispiox roadblock went up, and maybe they'll arrive in force at the Mill Creek Road blockade and at the Kitwancool River bridge. But they won't find Dimlahamid, even though the land claim, the roadblocks, the death feasts, even the very trees themselves showed evidence that we were all in the shadow of something that had something to do with the distant past and something to do with the distant future. All these centuries after the goats' feast, it was still bad luck among the Gitksan even to look at the clouded peak of Stegyawden, looming as it does over Old Town, New Town, Carnaby, Two Mile, Gitanmaax and Hagwilget. And it was in Stegyawden's shadow that a promised redrawing of the economic and political map of Canada's hinterland began with the slow pace through the Canadian courts of *Delgamuukw versus The Queen*.

The site of Dimlahamid/Dizkle is precisely where the Athapascan languages that begin in the bush country of northern Manitoba come to their western wall with the Wet'suwet'en language, and it is this place that marks the longitude on the North American map where the diverse and distinct languages of the west coast begin. As the rain fell into the campfire and 'Noola talked about the goats' feast on Stegyawden, what emerged was a deeper confluence than the joining of the two great rivers below the mountain that appears on B.C.'s map as Mount Rocher DeBoule. It was more than the confluence of the rivers the first people called the 'Ksan and the Wedzenkwe and the white people had come to call the Skeena and the Bulkley.

In all of North America it is only British Columbia's

northwest mountains that harbour that strange white bear the old Indians said could take the form of a man. The half-mythical bear was unknown to the outside world until 1905, when it was formally classified as *Ursus americanus kermodei* by the naturalist William Hornaday of the New York Zoological Society. A subspecies of the black bear, the Kermode is also known to take the colours red, orange and yellow. They are rarely seen these days, but there is a stuffed white Kermode, a car accident victim, that stands at the ready behind the mayor's chair in the municipal council chambers in Terrace, a few miles downriver from the Gitksan eagle clan's western frontiers.

Of the four major biogeoclimatic zones in Canada — arctic, northern, interior and coast — three of those zones (all but arctic) converge in the same valley bottoms where Dimlahamid is said to have existed. The coast zone follows the temperate rainforest in the shadow of the coastal mountain ranges from Alaska to California. It is rich in lush forests of hemlock, cedar, fir and alder that took root in the rotting carcasses of pioneering salmon that reclaimed their ancient spawning beds following the retreat of the last ice age 12,000 years ago. The interior zone begins in the Rocky Mountains and it follows their westward slopes to New Mexico, a cold-winter, hot-summer series of ecosystems that includes alpine tundra, sage grasslands and forests of pine, aspen and fir. The northern zone spreads a carpet of boreal forest from the northern coast mountains at Dimlahamid to Eurasia, interrupted briefly by the North Atlantic. It is tundra and muskeg, balsam, willow, birch and spruce.

This dramatic ecological confluence finds its way into Westar's sawmills and whole log chippers as something Dan Madlung, Westar's Carnaby general manager, likes to describe as Hemlock Surprise. It's a log that looks just fine. It's as solid as a hard block on one end and just as solid on the other, but in the middle it's pulp. "It's rotten," he complained one day from behind his desk at Carnaby. "It's the most rotten, decadent resource in the whole province." To Kenny Rabnett, the Suskwa homesteader who has worked so many long hours mapping the chiefs' territories and marking the boundaries of forest stands and clearcuts, it's a peculiar hybrid mix of different forest types that occurs nowhere else in nature.

The problem of finding Dimlahamid on the map of this transitional region between these three key planetary systems is that the trail disappears, reappears, and sometimes when it looks like it's just coming up on the outskirts, it disappears again over the height of land on the far mountain range.

On the Gitksan and Wet'suwet'en map, dozens of trails linked the winter villages and the summer villages with each of the resource-rich house territories within the 22,000-square-mile chiefs' confederacy. Anthropologist Richard Daly has identified 23 major trading trails linking the people of Dimlahamid with neighbouring peoples across a portion of the continent as large as Europe. The bush highways led north to the Sekani country of the Rocky Mountain Trench, west to the coast where the sea lanes were joined, north to regions above the Russian Fort Dionysis in what was to become Alaska, and south to the arid meadows of the Chilcotin country. A major thoroughfare connected the various Gitksan villages along the Skeena to the rich oolichan fishing grounds within Nisga'a territory to the north — an annual fishery that the Nisga'a hosted at the estuary of the Nass River involving fishermen from far-flung nations hundreds of miles in every direction. It is known as the Kitwancool Trail, and Daly says this about it: "As a hunting trail, it is undoubtedly many thousands of years old, but as a major trade route it probably came into importance between two and three thousand years ago." The road was cut a metre deep in places from heavy use. Charles Horetzky, a Scottish-born Ukrainian adventurer, Hudson's Bay Company official and explorer, travelled the Kitwancool Trail on a contract with the Canadian Pacific Railway in 1872, the year after B.C. joined Confederation. He encountered more than 100 travellers returning from a feast at Kitwancool, and he saw "not only the men, but also the women and children, laden with large cedar boxes, of the size and shape of tea chests, which were filled with the rendered grease of the candlefish … one savage had, in addition to the usual load of grease, perched on its summit, an old and decrepit woman, perhaps his mother."

There are other trails, from the far past, marked on the maps in the ada'ox and the kungax. Among the Gitksan there are stories of the travels of a group of brothers. They encounter a series of adventures on a great journey that takes them to the prairie provinces. There is another story about a strange visitor to Dimlahamid who befriends a chief's son. The two travel to heaven through a hole in the sky. Among the Wet'suwet'en there is the tradition of a trail that leads to the city of the dead. The journey begins with a grieving husband who wishes to travel with his wife to the land where the spirits live. The trail takes them over precipice and cataract and across rivers, and when they arrive in the city of ghosts they eat meals of snakes and lizards.

Maybe the archeologists who scoured these trails looking for signposts to Dimlahamid just hadn't seen them in what they found. Maybe it was there in something that had perplexed them, an aberration, a strangely carved stone, a maul or a mask, and maybe they had explained it away somehow. These things do happen, after all. It happened in 1979, when British archeologists had on their hands what they explained away as a "Victorian knife-sharpening stone" found three feet underground at the base of a wall in an English country garden. The object had been brought to London by a certain

Mr. C. H. Wallace of Grantham, Lincolnshire. It was later determined to be one of those mysterious stone batons that are unearthed from time to time in the Skeena River area, of the same style as those 35 stone batons Chief Johnny Muldoe found in 1898 at the depth of four or five feet in a clay-lined pit at Hagwilget. The Skeena River identity of Wallace's knife-sharpening stone was eventually discovered by the joint efforts of Donald Abbott of the B.C. Provincial Museum and Jonathan King of the Museum of Mankind in England. But they never did find out how a Skeena baton found its way to an English country garden in Lincolnshire.

And archeologist Charles Borden was never quite sure how to explain away a Sung dynasty coin, minted in China in 1125, which he found at the village of Chinlac on the Wet'-suwet'en chiefs' eastern frontiers. Borden notes that the village, part of which he excavated in 1951, was abandoned perhaps as early as 1745 but may have been occupied until the late eighteenth century. All he could say about the coin and the dentalium shells he found with it was that the people at Chinlac were engaged in a trade system with links to the coast.

That trade system flourished with links across the Bering Sea and through Asia, long before any other European powers visited North America's northwest coast, as the Russians first concluded in 1740. The Chukchis of Siberia traded through their tribal networks to the Inuit, the Aleuts and Tlingits of what is now Alaska, and iron was in the possession of coastal peoples long before any of them had seen white men. Centuries of Asian-North American trade flourished, and to this day, Alaska's St. Lawrence Island Yupik people count their cousins, uncles and aunts among the Chuckchi and Yupik of the Siberian Chukotsk and the Russian town of New Chaplino. When Europeans made their first contacts with the peoples of Canada's west coast, the Indians were no timid children of the forest who ran at the sight of high-masted frigates. It was July 20, 1774, when Captain Juan Perez, aboard the *Santiago*, failed for the fog and rain to find anchorage off the Duu Guusd region of what we now call the Queen Charlotte Islands. One of the two priests aboard the ship, Frey Juan Crespi, noted in his diary that three canoes approached the ship. In each of the Haida's cedar ocean-going canoes, the men were singing. In one canoe a man stood and danced, and spread birds' down on the water, a traditional gesture of welcome. They had iron-bladed axes and harpoons. They traded some trinkets for dried fish. The next day, 21 canoes approached the ship, and on board the canoes were more than 200 men, women, boys and girls. In a great flourish of singing, drumming and dancing, the fair continued. They traded knives, beads and cloth for beaver-pelt capes and quilts "sewed together so skilfully that no tailor could have done it better," and blankets of mountain goat wool "so closely woven that it seems to have been made on a loom." The diaries record that the people were beautiful and healthy, were it not for those horrible, shocking labrets.

In Dimlahamid, the women wore labrets, those palm-sized ornaments inserted into an incision in the lower lip, and enlarged over time, that have long confounded Grant Keddie of the B.C. Provincial Museum. Throughout the Gitksan territories, downriver to the coast and everywhere the ada'ox recounts the people of Dimlahamid migrating after the great snowfall, the women wore labrets. Labrets occur rarely and sporadically in the history of human societies on earth. They have occurred in Mesopotamia, the Balkan states and the Nile River area, which can be discounted as trailheads to Dimlahamid. But about 10,000 years ago, women of high rank in coastal societies around the Pacific started wearing labrets. The oldest are found in the southern harbours of the Siberian Kamchatka peninsula, and then they show up around Kodiak Island in Alaska about 5,000 years ago. On the other side of the Pacific, they become a bit of a fashion craze on the Japanese island of Hokkaido, and then they spread rapidly down the Canadian coastline, among the Gitksan, Haida, Heiltsuk and Salish shortly after they started showing up on the Aleutian Islands and among the Siberian Chukchis. Keddie says he reckons that the presence of labrets among the Gitksan and their neighbours provides "evidence that intensive trade-marriage interaction spheres involving extensive sea travel were present around the Pacific Rim 5,000 years ago," around the time of the advent of Dimlahamid. He says: "Cultural exchanges at this time played an important role along with local continuities in launching the developmental stage of cultures on the Northwest coast and possibly had an effect on those of Mesoamerica."

But looking for Dimlahamid on Asian maps doesn't help much more than looking for it on government forestry charts or Tourism B.C. roadmaps. The earliest Asian maps, hardly reliable by any contemporary standard, are found in the *Classic of Mountain and Seas*, compiled by a Chinese named Yu in 2025 BC. All that can really be said is that the countries he says he visited — by his charts, in the general vicinity of what was to become Canada's west coast — bear no resemblance to anything anywhere along the coast. But the Chinese were master mariners, and between the second and seventh centuries they had travelled the coasts of India, East Africa and Australia in ships with battened sails, leeboards and rudders. Somehow, as if only to annoy later white historians, Asian hookworm became a common parasitical infection among certain North American Indians, and somehow, Mexican maize found its way to Assam in India more than 700 years before Columbus.

In 1761, the French sinologist Joseph de Guignes found among Chinese imperial documents the account of Hwui Shan, an Afghani Buddhist who arrived in China in 450 AD and eight years later set off across the Pacific with eight other monks. The records of the first leg of their journey show a remarkably accurate diary of their voyages past the northern Japanese islands, the Kurile Islands and Kamchatka. Shan correctly places the Aleutian Islands on his charts, and then he arrives off the North American coast, or what de Guignes would have us believe is the North American coast, which Shan named the Great Han, or the Land of Rushing Water. He said the people had rude attitudes but a joyous approach to life. When he got back to China 40 years later, the empire was engulfed in war, and it was three years before he got a chance to tell his stories to the new emperor, Wu Ti. The emperor was interested only enough to ensure the story was written down. So much for finding Dimlahamid in the Land of Rushing Water.

It's true that all along North America's west coast, evidence of trans-Pacific trade has emerged over the years in coins, bamboo timbers, shipwrecks and pottery technology. And it's true the Nuu-Chah-Nulth on Vancouver Island's west coast have told stories of visits by men in ships, generations before Captain James Cook's landfall at Friendly Cove. The early seafarers were known, in literal translation, as the "eaters of maggots." In southwestern Alaska, 1,600-year-old Chinese metal pieces have been discovered in archeological digs at sites of the ancient Iputak people. At the time of Christ, copper ornaments were in use by the Gitksans' neighbours a few miles down the Skeena. By the twelfth century, metal objects of Asian origin were common throughout Alaska. On Saturna Island, off B.C.'s south coast, a young boy walking the beach in 1956 found a shard of earthenware in the shape of a human head, with a tuft of human hair attached and the jaw missing. Archeologist Don Abbott consulted the British Museum, where a study confirmed Abbott's conclusion that the piece was apparently of Asian origin and about 2,000 years old.

All this mysterious archeology really does is help to confirm a cultural continuum around the top of the North Pacific, one in which trade goods were diffused throughout, with a Chinese coin showing up every once in a while to illustrate the breadth of its trail networks. It helps to tilt the map on its axis just enough to see Dimlahamid/Dizkle in what is perhaps its more appropriate geographical context, one that includes Kamchatka on that side and Namu on this side, where at the time of the advent of Dimlahamid the women from one end of the continuum to the other started wearing labrets, and men started spearing animals with bilaterally barbed harpoons. It is what Simon Fraser University professor Roy Carlson describes as circum-Pacific drift, "a combination of small-scale diffusion and migration." The problem with tracking the diffusion since Dimlahamid is that it is "overshadowed in the archeological record by evidences of local cultural growth" and trade relations with other North American peoples. But the diffusion disposes of the map upon which Indian hunters chase some mammoths across the Bering land bridge, spread throughout North and South America, and sit around waiting to be discovered by Columbus. After years of studying Pacific coast cultures, Clement W. Meighan at the University of California at Los Angeles concluded: "Among the first settlers of the New World were people who were not comparable to the upper paleolithic hunters of the old world ... their ancestors are probably to be seen in the very early shell middens of Japan and Northern Asia."

But 'Noola and Haa'txw and Soup and Josh did not come from Japan. It would be nice if it were so easy. The fact is that nobody is really sure where they came from, and the best archeologists disagree amongst themselves about which direction the Gitksan came from when they arrived. There is the McDonald-Inglis argument, which is that the Gitksan culture came from the general direction of the coast, and that Gitksan culture as it had evolved by the time Horetzky walked the Kitwancool Trail was already in place about 1,500 years ago. Then there's the Ives-Rubel-Rosman argument that the Gitksan came downstream, or at least westward, from the interior bush country. Both sides of the debate seem to agree that the other may be at least partly right, with some downriver travel and some upriver travel.

One thing they all seem to agree on is summed up by Gary Coupland of the University of Toronto: Something happened on the Skeena River, beginning about 3,500 years ago. The Gitksan ada'ox recalls a great renaissance, a cultural flourishing following the wrath of the Medeek, the bear spirit, about that time. Coupland identifies that time as "a period of broadening resource diversity ... an important change in subsistence orientation toward riverine and forest efficiency." What that means to an archeologist is that all of a sudden there's chipped projectile points and formed bifaces and fish rack post molds all over the place.

And Coupland goes further than most have gone on the scientific trail to Dimlahamid. He says the people came from the coast, maybe 6,000 years ago, and whatever their far-distant origin, their immediate point of departure would appear to have been, maybe, Oregon, because there are three trails leading from that direction.

The first trail is obsidian. It's of volcanic composition, usually black, and it's like hard glass. When people first start showing up in Gitksan country, they're carrying obsidian, a top-dollar trading commodity used in the manufacture of microblades. South along the coast from the Skeena mouth, at Namu, archeologists have found an amazing mix of obsidian. There's buckets of obsidian at Namu. It was like a big microblade factory. Some of it comes from Anahim, about 140 miles across the mountains. There's also some obsidian there from Mount Edziza in the Stikine country, hundreds of miles north. And there's still more obsidian at Namu from Oregon, and the Oregon obsidian appears on B.C.'s coast about 6,000 years ago, at about the same time or a bit before the obsidian carriers show up in the vicinity of what was to become Dimlahamid.

The second trail leading from Oregon has to do with words. The Gitksan language, and its contiguous relatives, the Tsimshian and Nisga'a (both of which passed through Dimlahamid) form either a linguistic isolate, or fall within a little-understood linguistic group called Penutian. Nobody knows how Penutian speakers ended up around the Skeena and the Nass in British Columbia. Nobody else on earth speaks languages within that group except the Miwoks and Patwins of Oregon and California and their distantly related language-cousins, the Zuni, a pueblo people on the New Mexico-Arizona border.

The third trail traverses even more murky countryside, and it passes mainly through a peculiar marriage custom and a mortuary practice. There is an occasional matrilineal cousin-marriage custom approved in the Skeena-Nass country that appears among none of the 172 indigenous cultures of the North American west except the Miwoks and the Patwins. In the Nass and Skeena, there is also a custom strikingly similar to the California Penutians' ritual preparation of the corpse by the fathers' side of the family.

It's always been a mystery to anthropologists how a people can seem to just drop out of the sky like this. It doesn't happen often, but it happens. It happened in the Lake River Valley in Washington state, near the Columbia River estuary, about 600 years ago. Nobody knows where these people came from, but there they were, at about 1400 AD. They were potters and artisans, and they left behind the shattered bits of more than 200 ceramic figurines, bowls, tobacco pipes and pendants of the same type found in coastal Japan, North and South Korea and Siberia. "The remarkable thing about the Lake River ceramics is that they occur at all," says Alison Stenger of the U.S. Institute for Archeological Studies. None of the tribal groups in the area had any ceramic tradition. Nobody anywhere near the Washington coast had any tradition of ceramics. Stenger notes that the ceramic artifacts occur at about the same time as a migration of people from Japan, but as for the Lake River people, nobody knows where they came from or where they went.

There is another culture like that, one that seems to more or less appear out of nowhere at about the same time as the Lake River potters, but these people are still very much around. They are the Zuni, and even though they are among the ten most-documented of all peoples in anthropological literature, their origins remain the least understood. One person who has tried probably the hardest is Alaskan professor Nancy Yaw Davis, who says that to understand the Zuni we have to "reconsider concepts pertaining to the movement of ideas and people through time and space." The Zuni speak a language related to no other in North America except for a remote connection to the rare Penutian languages. The Zuni have distinctive tooth features and an unexplained high incidence of type B blood, putting them, genetically, closer to the Japanese than to any North American people. They just don't fit. The Zuni emerged as a people entirely distinct from their Pueblo, Papago, Tewa, Hopi and Pima neighbours in about the thirteenth century. In the late 1930s and 1940s, archeologists Carl Seltzer and Frank Roberts studied Zuni skeletal material and found evidence of "the arrival of a new element in the population," people completely different in body stature and cranial shape, in the thirteenth century. The Zuni recall that period in their history with ongoing visits to certain shrines in their homelands, commemorating a time that begins with migrations across the ocean to the desert. They remember the time with terror, and the oral tradition is rich in stories of storms at sea. Certainly a time of great upheaval in the Zuni homelands is well confirmed by the archeological record. They moved from place to place, they fortified their villages, started raising cotton and turkeys and making glazed pottery.

The Zuni believe that the country they occupy is the middle of the world. Their worldview arises from that notion, and it influences everything in their lives from the names they give to cardinal points and colours to the way they build their houses and arrange things in their houses. Their matrilineal clans are also focussed on direction from the middle. Linguists, anthropologists, archeologists, geneticists and ethnologists have come away from the Zuni scratching their heads because they went into the desert to study Indians and they came away with notes on the Japanese, from blood type to concepts like yin and yang to scores of words that match in both languages. The thirteenth century was also a time of great upheaval in Japan, with wars and invasions by Chinese and feudal warriors roaming the countryside and new religious movements arising, a prominent one being the Jodo movement, or Pure Land Buddhism. One of the prime concerns of the Jodo was finding the centre of the world, and Jodo's adherents were ruthlessly persecuted. Robert Lewis, the Zuni pueblo governor, figures that some of the Japanese may well have fled the country in boats rather than risk execution for their religious beliefs. Nancy Yaw Davis puts it this way: "I conclude the Zuni are distinct in language, culture, prehistory and biology partly because of relatively recent Japanese admixture."

Apart from the occasional shipwreck, religious exile or voyage of discovery, there wasn't much to disrupt the rich, stable interplay of cultural and economic interaction around the top of the North Pacific that began at about the time of the advent of Dimlahamid. From the northern islands of Japan to the northern California coast, a steady curving line of cultures thrived along the coastal rainforests and mammal-rich islands like an azimuth with its zenith somewhere around the eastern latitude of Dimlahamid. It was a great arc that began on the coast at what is now northern California, where Yurok priests led their congregations in elaborate first-salmon ceremonials involving obsidian swords, headdresses of pileated woodpecker and the skins of albino deer. The arc runs northwest, through dozens of national territories including the Tolowa, Quileute, Salish, Kwagewlth, Haisla and Haida, around the sea islands of the Tlingit, Eyak and Aleut to the Yupik, and then down the Siberian archipelago, past the Chukchis, the Kamchadals and the Kurile salmon fishermen to the Urupes, who traded nettle-woven goods for iron and cotton from the Japanese, who called them Jeso.

It did not end with the Dutch ship that traded among the Keek-Kuriles in 1643, and it did not end in 1733 when the Russian czar commissioned the first great expedition of white people among the peoples of Kamchatka and Alaska. The arc remained intact, and its trade routes were steady conduits of exotic commodities long after Vitus Bering's expedition of 1741. The trails leading to and from Dimlahamid were linked with more trails, and by the 1770s Aleut leaders were walking the streets of Saint Petersburg, marveling at the architecture after obtaining injunctions against the excesses of private-sector Russian traders in their island homelands. By the nineteenth century, hundreds of Nuu-Chah-Nulth fishermen from villages like Hesquiat and Ahousat were roaming the North Pacific in sealing schooners, returning home with rib-

ald stories about the tea houses of Yokohama. The arrival on
the scene of the Russians, Spanish, British and Americans
precipitated great economic booms, old trade compacts were
strengthened, rivalries were inflamed, wars and rebellions
broke out, peace was negotiated and hundreds of thousands
died of diseases the newcomers brought with them.

"Don't make fun of those visitors," is what the woman said
to her son, who came into the house with reports that the
strange men camped outside Dimlahamid were eating grass.
"Don't make fun of other people," 'Noola remembered the
woman had said.

Josh and Soup had gone to bed, and the rain was falling
heavily. Haa'txw sat quietly and listened as 'Noola continued
the story about the goats' feast.

"And the people got up and left to go to the feast and they
went on a road, and it looked very nice to them, but they
were really walking up that mountain, away from Dimlahamid. The mountain is Stegyawden, and they all came up to
the feast, and they sat in the feast hall. It was a big rock, but
it looked like a house to them. They sat for a long time. I
don't know how long they sat, but it's disrespectful at a feast
to get up and start asking questions."

'Noola was quiet. He couldn't quite remember the details
of what happened next, but it involved the appearance of the
mythical one-horned goat of Stegyawden, and his appearance
at the feast house is followed by a massacre of the guests,
whose bodies end up in heaps at the bottom of the mountain.

The boy who had painted the goat kid with ochre years
earlier was spared, protected by the goat kid, whose face still
bore the ochre mask he had painted.

"There is something about how during the night, a one-
horned goat rammed the house. But this man, this goat, said,
'I saved you because you had respect for me, and these other

people, when they killed us, they didn't show respect. That's why we had to take revenge.' The one-horned goat part, that's kind of hazy. But the whole feast house would shake."

Later that night, the rain stopped falling. 'Noola and Soup and Josh had climbed into their sleeping bags and Haa'txw, old Ernie Muldoe, talked about his days in California, the years he spent hunched over the rows of vegetables and about the friends he had made among the Mexicans. Just why he left Gitksan country and ended up in California was never clear, but it sounded like it had something to do with a love that had gone wrong. Before I turned in for the night he wanted to make a point about how his people, the Gitksan frogs, had come to settle at Dimlahamid.

"We originate from down on the coast, by the Tsimshians. They were overpopulated, I guess. There was one guy who was lazy, and he sits on a stump and just picks up the rotten fish that people throw away, and he kind of lives a hobo's life. He lived under a big stump, day in and day out. Then all of a sudden, he sees a beautiful lady in white, and the lady talks to this man, and she says, 'Why do you live this way?' and he says, 'I can't help it. I'm a poor person.'

"She says to him, 'What do you crave to eat?' and he said meat and stuff, whatever. So she came back and laid a table for him and brought him beautiful clothes. And the people said, 'What the heck? What's going on here?'

"He followed the lady to this little pond, and he found her. She was a beautiful stork and she was eating frogs. She eventually told him, 'Why don't we live together and we will have some children,' and he said, 'I'm not good enough.' She wanted to, though, and so they went upriver, they followed up the Nass River, and they had children, and they had more children and kept going upriver, and had more children. But the children, he worried that they would be inbred, so she made the frog tribe, then the wolf, the fireweed and the eagle. The man said, 'What's the idea of that?' and she said it was so that the frog will marry the wolf, or the eagle, like that. The frog was the first one she called out. That's her food, too, I guess. They came to Gitwangak, to Skeena Crossing, then Gitanmaax, then Kisgegas, Kuldoe, Bear Lake, all the places, as each couple got married."

Haa'txw emptied what was left of his coffee into the fire. The camp was dark and quiet, except for the low roar of the Bulkley below the ridge. Somewhere on the far side of the river, a train rumbled slowly through the mountains.

EIGHT

VICTORIA COMES TO THE SUSKWA

The world was beginning to close in on Dimlahamid and the days were blurring into each other with new developments on the roadblock front, tactical advances and meetings and war councils and rumours. One thing was sure: the Gitksans' war-on-the-ground strategy was escalating in ways the B.C. government didn't like, and something was coming to a head, and what was also sure was that Soup Wilson, his arms wrapped around the steering wheel of his old Ford van, was roaring through the night down the Yellowhead Highway at speeds much greater than common sense would normally permit. He was leaning forward in the driver's seat, squinting into the white column his headlights lit up in the rain on the road ahead. The wipers slapped the rain furiously back and forth across the windshield, inches from his face.

The terrain was changing rapidly. Allegiances were shifting, and the urgency of the situation was bringing some of the white people on side. The chiefs' spokesmen were meeting with the loggers somewhere out there and we had forgotten where we were supposed to be.

At Gitsegukla we turned off the highway and bashed our way over the rutted dirt roads asking anyone who had the bad luck to be out walking and in the way of the muddy water Soup's wheels splashed in sheets from the potholes. No meeting here. Soup pulled out onto the Yellowhead again and raced off in the direction of Gitwangak, nose to the windshield, and in another half-hour we made it to Gitwangak. There were a few pickup trucks parked outside the elementary school, and when we stumbled into the library everybody was sitting on children's chairs, laughing at us and pointing to our feet. We looked down and saw our boots, and behind us were two tracks of mud leading from the door down through the hall. Soup looked at his boots. His eyes glanced back down the hall. He looked at everyone else's feet, looked up at me, and everybody started laughing again.

There was something of a mixup. The logging contractors didn't get word of the meeting and the only one who showed was Brian Larson, Soup's boss on that thinning job on the Suskwa before the roadblock shut him down. There was Kitwancool band chief Glen Williams, Sgenna, Peter Turley, Mas Gak, Mark Duivan (the tribal council's Ottawa lobbyist), Yagosip, Gordon Sebastian, Marvin George and a few others. The laughing died down and they got back to the discussion.

The road from here to saltwater at Stewart is paved now, and 1.3 million cubic metres of wood is leaving over that road each year to be dumped whole in the water for export to Japan with some going to the southern coastal mills. It's wood the chiefs want left in their territories, it's wood the loggers would like to cut, and it's wood Westar would like for its mills. There's a consensus emerging.

"We're in the best position in this room to stop that," said Mas Gak. "The workers can't do that. The contractors can't do that. We can do it, the chiefs and the house members."

Brian Larson piped up. "Everybody knows that in the next ten to fifteen years there's going to be nothing left. But they've got today to look at. In the back of their minds they have their payments, their houses, their kids. They could all be out of their houses tomorrow."

Everybody got a word in, had their say, drank some coffee and ate a few cookies. They left with a plan to meet again, this time with the union representatives in the lunch room at the Gitwangak sawmill in a day or two.

When Mas Gak showed up at that meeting, the consensus was even more solid. Joe Mallia, the truck loggers' representative for the International Woodworkers of America, put it this way: "The guys say it doesn't matter to them where they haul logs. But the time is going to come when there won't be any logs to haul anyplace. It's that simple. Because there just won't be any logs. We're exporting our own jobs." Surinder Malhotra, the IWA's business agent for the millworkers (most of the Gitwangak millhands are Gitksan) had a broad smile on his face when the meeting ended. His idea was for another Indian blockade, maybe up at Meziadin Junction. There wouldn't be a stick of timber leaving the province's entire northwest quarter. "Sure," he said. "A blockade. Nothing moves. Everything stops."

The plan was to get everybody together this time, the chiefs, their house members, the loggers and millworkers, their union representatives, and Westar's local managers. On Tuesday, at Gitwangak hall.

There was nothing much to do now but wait for what was going to happen next. Mas Gak and the George brothers and

Gordon Sebastian spent the hours finishing off a two-by-four-and-plywood gatehouse at the Suskwa roadblock. All that was missing now was a gate for the road, maybe something you could pull up and let down from the gatehouse. There was steelhead in the river and firewood to be cut. The bush camp was lively again, with the women cooking meals and the men trying to look busy but mostly just telling stories and cleaning their rifles.

While the battle lines outside were slowly forming, Sebastian was rolling over a sidehill on a dirt track about twenty miles in from the Suskwa blockade when he spotted Vernon Joseph's pickup truck rumbling along the narrow rut through the willow scrub up ahead. With him was Duivan, the tribal council's lobbyist. The two of them were out hunting, but it soon became clear to Sebastian that they were hoping to find him as much as the grouse they were after. Joseph, Daakhluumgyet since Elsie's feast, accelerated and slammed on his brakes at Sebastian's front bumper. Gordon jumped out. This was a challenge, after all. Daakhluumgyet jumped out his side and the two started mock-punching and wrassling. Duivan got out and the jokes turned to the rebel-held zones and the fluke of such a chance meeting so deep within the liberated territory, and then he gave Sebastian the news.

In Ottawa, Indian Affairs Minister Pierre Cadieux was getting ready to get on a plane for Victoria to meet with his provincial counterpart, Jack Weisgerber, and with Attorney-General Bud Smith. The Gitksan campaign was expected to be front and centre on the backroom agenda. At that moment Weisgerber's deputy minister, Eric Denhoff, was on his way up, booked at the Hudson Bay Lodge in Smithers, and he was expected out first thing next morning at the roadblock, by himself. The last thing the government needed was a dramatic dustup between Mounties and Indians that would draw attention to the government's forest-mining policies, to say nothing of its policies towards Indians. So Denhoff was on his way for some last-ditch try at a low-key truce.

And Daakhluumgyet had just cornered Sebastian into setting everything up, which was the last thing he needed. Gordon was hoping to get back into Hagwilget to pick up Shirley and the kids to bring them to Terrace, where he had a regional board meeting. It was supposed to be a break for them. The kids could go swimming or something. Shirley would be steamed, for sure, but he gets called on like this. He's a lawyer, after all, and a Gitksan frog to boot. During the last provincial election he got talked into running as an independent for the Gitksan. So this sort of thing happens from time to time.

He ended up spending the rest of the morning roaring around in his Bronco four-by-four trying to get the word out that the government was coming for a meeting at the Suskwa camp first thing Saturday morning, and all the chiefs had to be there. When we got to Yagosip and Sgenna's house in the Birch Grove reserve subdivision just outside Gitanmaax, Yagosip was in the kitchen. "I'm just putting in my apples," she said, busy boiling jars. Gordon filled her in and roared off. We stopped by Xsimwits'iin's house in Gitanmaax and met up with Karen Morrison. "He's working nights," she said. "And all the elders have gone to Reno."

"You let him know," Gordon said, pulling out on the road down into Hazelton. After getting tied up notarizing documents he sat behind his desk at the Gitksans' community law office and got back to working the telephones for the next morning's meeting. Outside, an RCMP cruiser pulled into the parking lot to break up a crowd of old men hooting and singing between slugs from a big bottle of red wine. By nightfall, Sebastian had got word to everyone who was at least in the territories, and after he commiserated with Shirley after dinner about the day's changed plans we headed out from Hagwilget back to the camp. Turning the wide bend in the paved road that circles the reserve, our headlights picked out a body lying in the road. Gordon slammed on his brakes and swerved. We skidded to a stop.

We backed up and jumped out of the car. The young man in the road lay still, but he was breathing. He started to move his legs, and as we knelt beside him a teenaged girl ran out from the dark. "Don't hurt him," she shouted. "Leave him alone." We helped him to his feet. He staggered. No, he said, I haven't been hit. He reeked of wine. The girl wept, walked toward us and threw her arms around the young man. She helped him off the road and they stumbled off together into the dark. "Why did you do that?" she was asking him. "What are you trying to do?"

If it hadn't been so dark, from where the two of us were left standing on the road we probably could have seen the huge cross in the Hagwilget graveyard. The life-sized, gold-painted Christ hangs there from his giant crucifix, looking down on the sad, fallen crosses and wooden headstones. Only a few years had gone by since a skinny twenty-year-old kid named Joey Pierre, a frog, hanged himself from that cross. He hadn't had much of a life, but things had been looking up for him. He had a girlfriend and he was training as a chef, but something went wrong. He told his friends he was going to kill himself, but nobody believed him. When the village woke up the next morning, there he was, dead on the cross.

Two years later, Joey's aunt Amelia hanged herself in the basement of her broken-down house in the village. The house sat empty until Gordon's cousin Johnny moved in, but one day last summer Amelia's widowed husband Jack stopped by for a visit and he found Johnny dead. He had died of pneumonia, and the drinking probably helped it along.

The kid on the road didn't die that night. Maybe it was the timing that was wrong, or maybe he was just lucky that Gordon was quick on the brake pedal.

On the road out to the Suskwa the night sky was shimmering with the northern lights, hanging in a delicate aurora curtain between the snow-capped mountains. The old people said if you whistled, the curtains would move towards you. A crescent moon rose from behind the high peaks to the northeast, and when we got back to camp, Sgenna was there, carving circles in the dirt in front of the campfire with a big blunt axe.

He wasn't impressed with the idea of the meeting with the government.

"So now we're going to talk to this new Indian agent tomorrow about whether or not we're going to open up the road again. For what? A bag of rice? A bag of sugar? I don't need no sugar. I don't need no rice."

Sgenna's a big man with a heavy face and a crewcut. He's 57, and his wife Yagosip is a key chief in the Suskwa house territories. He has mouths to feed and a 1977 Kenworth logging truck with a brand new 400 Cummins diesel engine and $43,000 owing on it and he says he's ready to lose it all if that's what the chiefs want. As long as the roadblock's up, he's not going to haul logs. He'll park it. "I want to stand beside the chiefs at this blockade," he used to say. He was clearly not in much of a mood to engage some senior bureaucrat from Victoria in a pleasant conversation about the affairs of the world. The last of that type to get close to Sgenna was Forests Minister Dave Parker, who had come to Hazelton a few months earlier for a ceremonial planting of the millionth tree in the provincial government's reforestation program, a scheme that serves as much a public relations function as an effective silvicultural regime. Sgenna had walked up to Parker — both are big, imposing men — and in front of a crowd of local dignitaries and a handful of news reporters, placed his hand on the minister's shoulder and said: "I'm going to give you a name. An Indian name." Parker beamed. "From now on this man shall be known as Chief Walking Eagle." Parker was beside himself. It was almost too good to be true. "And you know what that means. He's so full of shit he can't fly." Parker winced.

Gordon reminded Sgenna of that day and Delbert cheered up. Soon he was spinning yarns like the one about the day Jimmy Morgan climbed hand over hand on the Gitwangak ferry cable right across the Skeena River, because the ferry man was asleep.

"His hands were meat. He'd stop and rest and hang from his feet, but he made it eventually, by golly," Sgenna laughed. He told another story or two. He tried to make us laugh, and he tried to make himself laugh, but it wasn't working very well.

There still wasn't much of a mood for jokes the next morning when Eric Denhoff parked his rental car at the Suskwa road bridge across the Bulkley River, on the public side of the roadblock, and walked the rest of the way over in his sparkling white Reeboks and yellow rainslicker. He's in his mid-40s, he's sharp, and he had just the skills needed by the party in power when *Delgamuukw versus The Queen* started attracting attention to the B.C. government's shadowy Indian policy. Denhoff comes from a newspapering family, and his skills are in public relations. He was a reporter himself for a while in Alberta, where he ended up with Harold Cardinal's Indian Affairs department. B.C. Premier Bill Vander Zalm is particularly publicity-conscious, and he loves good Indian publicity. There's nothing better for a right-wing politician than to be seen with friendly Indians, and that's exactly how Vander Zalm began his 1986 provincial election campaign.

That was back when B.C.'s Indians had hopes that this buck-the-establishment Social Crediter might actually change B.C.'s 120-year-old position on Indian land title. So Vander Zalm kicked off his campaign by spending the night in a Musgamagw Indian village at Kingcome Inlet. It was something the Indians there said they regretted doing almost as soon as Vander Zalm left.

The hands-on work was Denhoff's job. If it was an application for funds for an Indian women's transition house in Vancouver, Denhoff dealt with it and made sure the government came out looking good. If the government granted a woodlot licence to an Indian band so they could sell some timber out of a valley they'd called home for centuries, Denhoff issued the press release. If Indians set up a roadblock somewhere, Denhoff's the man the RCMP would call. The native affairs ministry had expanded since it was first set up as a secretariat only a few years earlier (B.C. has no legislative authority for Indians), and its main objective on every front is to dissuade Indians from pursuing aboriginal title or asserting their rights in the courts or otherwise. The latest initiative on that front was the Premier's Council on Native Affairs. It raised hopes in Indian communities from Gitlakdamix to Tobacco Plains, but it had become what most Indian leaders had feared: more photo opportunities for the premier and a series of opportunities to use Indians as press-conference backdrops. The Gitksans were wise to this sort of thing. So when Denhoff had dodged the puddles on the track from the roadblock into the camp, it was right down to business.

Around the fire sat Josh McLean, Soup Wilson, 'Noola, Axtiizeex (Bruce Johnson), Marvin George, Djogaslee (Walter Wilson), Yagosip, Sgenna and their grandson Corey, Haa'txw, Mas Gak, Gord Sebastian, Wii Muugalsxw (Art Wilson), his wife Kathy Holland, and his son Jody. In one way or the other, all ten houses with territories within the Suskwa watershed were represented around the fire.

Everybody said good morning.

"Well," said Mas Gak. "Let's get started."

He let Denhoff know right off the top that the chiefs were not interested in committees, joint-venture clearcutting, economic development funds or government grants.

"The issue here deals with the land," he said. "The jurisdiction on the land, the ownership of the land. Our main concern is the way the Crown is using the land."

Mas Gak set out the two immediate concerns that provoked the Suskwa roadblock that had, for almost a month, prevented access to hundreds of square miles of forest to all but Gitksans, Wet'suwet'ens, a handful of local residents and "friendlies," non-natives with special $10 fishing and hunting permits issued by the chiefs. Those concerns were the export of resources from the territories — sometimes out of the area, and sometimes out of the country entirely — and the matter of forest practices: clearcutting, steep slope logging, highgrading, soil erosion and generally bad management. Mas Gak reviewed the regional forest economy in detail and laid out specific complaints about forest practices. Most of the valley bottoms were being stripped of their best timber, over-harvesting continued throughout the vast Kispiox timber supply area, harvested timber was underutilized in the local mills, and the government had done nothing to encourage initiatives among the major players in the forest industry to draw greater value from the wood they consumed. The impact of government forest policies was compounded by restricted hunting, largely as a result of a lottery system for game animals that shut out the Gitksans, and the destruction of traplines, caused by the elimination of fur-bearer habitat by clearcut logging.

"We had to see that people appreciate the facts," Mas Gak said. "If the government didn't move, it was up to us to move."

Denhoff listened intently. When Mas Gak finished he said, "I appreciate the motivation you have." Denhoff said the province was concerned about value-added forestry, and the government would be interested in the Indians' concerns, and the premier and cabinet were very interested in what the Indians had to say. Of course the government's position on ownership and jurisdiction was well-known and nothing could be done about that, but perhaps if everybody sat down and talked things over, everybody might be able to get somewhere.

There was a long silence. Axtiizeex broke it.

"Myself," he said, stuffing his hands into the pockets of his blue ski jacket, "I don't like to see this going on if it causes hardship to people working on my territory. We have to live side by side here. These guys, I don't want to see them suffer hardship. They have to pay for their equipment. We know these things. I've worked 25 years falling myself, but I've been sitting around for the last five years now.

"I don't like to slash burn. Mother Nature has her own way of reviving the forests. These little animals, the squirrels, they have their own way of reviving it. I guess about these forest companies, I'd like to see them have more respect on our land."

Then Sgenna spoke, and Sgenna said what he usually said.

"If the chiefs say don't blockade, I don't blockade. But we have to blockade. I also have mouths to feed."

Kathy Holland stood up.

"I am in the house of Gyetm Guldoo. We will decide how to best use the resources on that house territory. We don't want anybody to go in there and do anything, as far as the involvement of the provincial government is concerned. We don't want anybody. Not from DIA, not from the forests ministry, nobody. We want to give the land some peace for a while. It's been ravaged too hard, for too long, and we want to give it some rest."

She stopped speaking, looked around quickly and said: "That's where I stand with it."

Then 'Noola spoke. He explained that he is from the House of Xsimwits'iin, which is also the House of Ludkudzii Wus, and Ludkudzii Wus is the "autocrat" in the house. Then he said: "It's been going on for too long. The government has just overlooked the needs of the Indians and now the white people are crying out about their needs."

Marvin George, a Wet'suwet'en leader and formerly the tribal council's cartographer, said his piece. "You want to compromise and get all the non-native people back to work, without addressing our concerns. If there's going to be logging, it will be under our jurisdiction."

The same stance was held by each speaker, until it came time for Denhoff to speak again, and it was more or less the same thing he said before, except this time he was a little bit on the snappy side. He talked about co-operation, joint ventures, resource conflict resolution processes that other Indians were involved with, and of course there was Tanizul Timber, which happened to be owned by Indians, and Tanizul held a provincial tree farm licence in Carrier territory northeast of the Wet'suwet'en country, and maybe the Gitksans would like to meet with the Premier's Council on Native Affairs, and maybe they'd like a joint Indian-government task force on forest use. But there would be no talking about the land claim. After all, that was before the courts.

"Land claim?" Sgenna perked up. "Whose land claim? Who is claiming the land? This is our territory. We're not claiming the land."

Denhoff was silent.

Mas Gak took a deep breath. He pointed out to Denhoff

that the forests ministry had selected several options for crossing the Babine River into the untouched northern territories. One site was Sam Green Creek, which was successfully blockaded during the summer. The other was Gail Creek, which the government was pushing towards before that route was closed with the Suskwa blockade. The other was Nikitkwa, in the Carrier territories.

"You can't keep ignoring us," Mas Gak said. "The day has come for the government to accept that. The judges say, 'If you own the land, why don't you act like you own the land?' But when we act, we're attacked. There has to be a shift in thinking. And we're going to do that. And the only way we see it happening is to do it ourselves. The ideal thing is if the provincial government pulls out of the court case. Right now."

There was another long silence. Sgenna drew a circle in the ground with a stick.

"We are the government here," he said. "The chiefs are. We have Gitksan law, and our law says if we warn you to stay off our land, we warn you once. We warn you again. And that's the last time. The next time, we kill you. You're dead."

This put a bit of a damper on the discussions. 'Noola tried to draw Denhoff out on his personal feelings about what he had heard from them, and what the chiefs had said about how they still owned the land. Denhoff was annoyed by that, and he complained that he was being backed into a corner of some kind. The meeting was running out of steam, so Mas Gak and Gordon Sebastian offered to take him for a drive up the Suskwa road to show him why they set up the blockade. On the way out, Roger Bealam, a sportsfisherman from Palm Beach, Florida, bought a $10 fishing permit from Gordon while Denhoff, whose government normally issued such permits, sat waiting in the car.

Mas Gak pointed out the clearcut hillsides, the huge patches of virgin timber hauled out of the valley, and the patch logging that had been cut in the 1970s and never replanted. Later on, back at the Bulkley bridge, it was obvious the tour hadn't much improved Denhoff's mood.

"We're getting phonecalls," he said. "Complaints. From hunters, from industry, concerned residents in the area. I think if we've got a job as a government, it's to balance all these views and find a way through it. So I'll go back and see what Jack [Weisgerber] has to say about setting up a task force or something along those lines. Then I'll call these guys back and see if anybody here's interested in it. The chiefs are saying that they want to see whether there's any seriousness on the part of the government. Or we could exchange injunctions."

While Denhoff was meeting with the chiefs, the forests ministry was quietly preparing another sale of timber in the already-ravaged Kispiox timber supply area, this time a sale of timber for pulpwood, over and above what the forests ministry had determined to be a safe, allowable annual cut. Also unknown to the chiefs at the time was the fact that the ministry was reviewing an application from Stege Logging, the owner of a long-closed sawmill that Westar once owned in South Town, for sawlogs in the same timber supply area, again over and above the allowable annual cut. The chiefs could say what they wanted; the government had its own plans.

Wii Muugalsxw had been pretty quiet during the meeting with Denhoff, but then he's usually pretty quiet. We walked to the middle of the Bulkley bridge, watched the river rolling beneath us in the autumn sunshine and talked about the Kispiox blockade back in the spring of 1988. Wii Muugalsxw said he figured, particularly after meeting with Denhoff, that maybe it was time for another one.

I remembered walking with him two years earlier through the rolling hills of the house territory entrusted to him through his name under Gitksan law. It was a good spring morning. His house territory lies square in the middle of what shows on the forest ministry charts as the Kispiox timber supply area. I remembered the sun was on the mountains when we left the village that morning, and the air was thick with the sweet smoke from the grass fires the people set to green up the hillsides. And I remembered walking with him through those hills, and how two-thirds of his territory lay barren and scarred from the valley floor to the snow-capped mountains. It was strewn with fallen timber, and I remembered how despairing he'd been back then, how his boots dug into the crusted snow as he followed the moose tracks in the shaded sidehills, how he stopped and said that he didn't know what to say about it, but he mainly felt hurt.

That was almost two years back, and now there was even less standing timber on his territory.

When you think about it, it probably is time for another roadblock up there, he said, kicking stones from the bridge into the river passing below. But there were people in his village to think of, and people in his family, and as a Kispiox wolf chief he had deeper responsibilities still. It was no easy choice.

There was his brother-in-law, Philip, for instance. Pictures of his eight children covered the walls in his house. Eight mouths to feed, Philip said, then there's the granddaughter in the house, and it's fair money hauling lumber off the house territory Wii Muugalsxw is entrusted to take care of and fair money is hard to turn down when you've got eight kids and a Grade 9 education.

Just how the day-long Kispiox blockade came to an end in 1988 wasn't a particularly pleasant subject of conversation for Wii Muugalsxw. That roadblock more or less fell apart, he remembered, kicking another rock into the river. There was all that talk about how someone might get hurt if the loggers are stuck there on the road in their trucks all night. When Wii Muugalsxw got back to the roadblock after a brief rest at his log house in the village the blockade was gone, and he thought maybe that's what had happened, that somebody had been hurt, or somebody had decided that somebody was going to get hurt, so it was taken down.

"I didn't like that," he said. "I didn't like the way it happened. We knew when we put up the blockade. We knew all along that somebody might get hurt. But everything fit, and I thought that's what it was."

But it wasn't. Dave Webster had promised Sgenna that he and the other truckloggers stuck on the inside of the blockade would come back to the feast hall to meet with the chiefs if they'd just move Robert Jackson's cedar log out of the way. The log got moved, but the loggers never showed up, and despite the high spirits of the day, the way it ended was what everyone remembered. Still, there's that meeting coming up in Gitwangak, and now that Elsie's feast is past there's talk of a meeting of the chiefs with territories in the Kispiox Valley, Wii Muugalsxw said. So there's something to look forward to, anyway.

We walked back to the camp. The betting around the fire was that the B.C. attorney-general's office would have its injunction to remove the Suskwa roadblock signed, sealed and ready from B.C. Supreme Court by the coming Thursday, and once everyone had agreed on what they were up against they headed out of camp and on about their business. Josh McLean sat alone up at the roadblock. Just as Wii Muugalsxw and Kathy said their goodbyes, Soup Wilson's van rumbled through the trees and out jumped Soup with a steelhead he'd just hooked from that favourite bend of his up on the Suskwa River. While all the big chiefs and the important people were talking around the bushcamp fire, Soup had slipped away and gone fishing.

"When I'm out in the bush, I got no worries," Soup said, hanging his fresh-caught fish from a willow tripod. "I feel free out there." He sat down, waving goodbye to Wii Muugalsxw and Kathy. "Nothing to worry about. Summertime, climb mountains. Beautiful-looking mountains. Just like a paradise. Beautiful flowers. You look down into the valleys. Beautiful. There's lots of things to do in the bush."

He poured himself a cup of coffee, looked around and saw that just about everyone had gone. He smiled.

Soup was born in the bush on an August morning in 1941, at a little lake near the old village of Caribou Hide. His parents were trappers and he's spent most of his life in the bush. His dad bought a house in Hazelton and Soup, the oldest of six children — two brothers, Moe and Danny, and three sisters, Mary, Rhoda and Gracie — went to school for the first time when he was eight. He stayed in school for three years, long enough to learn that all things being equal he'd just as soon be out in the bush. Soup grew up packing on the old Babine Trail, by horse and dog. Now he had a wife in Terrace ("Boy, does she love to play bingo") and he worried about his oldest, seventeen-year-old Alexander, and he wished the boy hadn't started smoking. Then there was fifteen-year-old Joey and thirteen-year-old Melissa and eleven-year-old Peter and Veronica, the nine-year-old he still called "the baby," and here was Soup catching steelhead and shooting grouse for people who might be described as people who put him out of a job. But they were people he would stand beside as long as they fed him, as he was fond of saying.

We sat and watched the fire. I thought about the government's next move, the chiefs' next move and where the loggers and millworkers would end up in the immediate scheme of things. Soup wasn't much interested. It was exciting and he was for it, but he didn't much bother about the details. Every once in a while a bush mouse scurried through the dirt.

"You go up in the mountains," Soup said, "and they're red. The mice. They're all red. It's the only place you see them. In the mountains."

He watched his fish, stared into the fire, and watched his fish a while more. Then he turned and pointed to the north.

"On the other side of that mountain, that sharp mountain." I looked where he was pointing, but there were no mountains to be seen through the thick stand of trees so I just imagined which one he meant. "We went up there and we seen them caribou horns. Old, old horns. Must be they've been there a long time. I think maybe they're still around. The odd one."

Deep inside the flames a rock cracked with a loud pop. And then there's just the sound of the Bulkley River hissing below the bridge.

"But I like goat hunting still," he said. "I used to be good at heights, eh? But I'm scared of heights now."

He still traps. His trapline is in the upper reaches of the Skeena. The frogs owned it once, but at some point far back in history the wolves shed blood on it, so it belongs to the wolves. Soup's father, a wolf, held it until he died, but he willed it to Soup, so now it's in the hands of the frogs again.

"Okay," Soup said. He pulled his mackinaw jacket closer under his chin and stretched out his legs. "Okay. I'll tell you a bullshit story.

"There's a guy named Arthur Harkin and he forgets his bullets, only finds one bullet, and he saw a grizzly bear and then he saw a bull moose standing there. So he grabbed his knife and he put it on the end of his barrel there and it split the bullet right in half and he got both of them."

A broad grin creased Soup's face.

"One time there I was up on the mountain and I threw

some rocks at a blue grouse trying to hit him and I heard a rockslide below me. I saw a big grizzly bear coming. A big bugger. And I did this."

Soup closed his eyes, jutted out his jaw, pursed his lips and emitted a very strange noise. Like a whistle.

"He stopped when I did that. He was about fifteen feet away. Then I shot him. My partner was behind me with a big axe. The bear, there was a big hole right between his eyes. They offered me $500 for the hide. That's, let's see, quite a few years ago. I was still single then. I was about 21 years old, I think. No, I was nineteen at the time.

"Another time I hit one grizzly, but just in the arm. He just bit his arm, and then he took off.

"At Kisgegas, me and my dad. I was pretty small. My dad shot this grizzly and he just wounded it. He buried himself in the moss, just waiting for us on the trail. So we had to circle around it. The next day we circled around and we saw him on the trail there, and his head was sticking out, and there was a little mouse, like those red ones, on top of his head. That's how we knew he was dead."

NINE

THE 'WATSX COMES TO THE SUSKWA

On Sunday morning, we stumbled through the deep moss into the dark spruce and hemlock forest about twenty miles into the high country, up in the headwaters of the Kispiox River. It was about three miles above the canyon where the Nangeese River comes out of the trees, almost as high as the alpine where the mountain goats live.

We found the image painted on a panel set deep in an ancient hemlock, recessed in a sort of natural alcove formed by the tree's own growth over about 200 years. In charcoal and oolichan grease were two large round eyes, set in an ovoid face, and the eyes stared out of the tree into the forest. In the swaying shafts of light that broke through the green old-growth canopy high above us, we could just make out on the breast of the image a u-shaped design, from which six hooked loops were suspended, three on each side of the u-form. Its hands were obscured, partly with the withering of the winters and partly by the thick bark of the tree that had grown around it.

A surveyor had come across it. The new logging road was just a short walk away. The provincial museum wanted it, but Walter Harris, Geel, was here with 21 members of his family, making something of a Sunday family outing of the business, to see that if it had to come down, he would see to it himself, and it would not be carted off to some museum.

And it had to come down. It was quite clear that the tree was rotten and dying, and it wouldn't last many more winters.

So Howard Sexsmith and Chuck Heit, Yaya, bound the tree with a thick rope, coiling it around the trunk about ten feet from the ground to prevent the tree from splitting halfway into the cut. Sexsmith fired up his chainsaw, cut a wedge from the north side of the tree, in the direction the image's eyes were staring, and after we all took cover he began the main cut from behind. When the tree finally fell and the ground stopped shaking, Sexsmith hollered, "It's safe," and we all crowded around. It was hollow for most of its length. Andy Reviakin, a student at the Forestry Technology Training Program, a school initiated by the Gitksan chiefs, reckoned the age at somewhere between 250 and 500 years, but it was just too hard to say. The rot was too far along and it was impossible to count the growth rings.

Sexsmith sawed another cut at the base of the tree well below the image panel, and after planning it all out and clearing what we could of a path, it took twelve of us to push the stump over on its side, and it took all of us every bit of an hour's worth of pushing and heaving, using smaller limbed trees as rollers, to get the hollow stump out through the moss to the logging road and into the back of Walter's pickup.

"I'm going to take it home and do what I can to save it. Preserve it," he said.

It sat in the back of his pickup truck, massive and heavy, making the truck look tiny and frail under the weight of it. The eyes of the image now stared skyward. We sat around a fire and drank tea and ate smoked salmon and wondered about it. It was a bit of a mystery. It may have been a boundary marker for Geel's house, since it was in the vicinity of the frontier of several house territories, and boundary markers were a common practice among Gitksan and Wet'suwet'en house chiefs. But they weren't generally so elaborate. There was agreement among Geel's family that it was a good thing, anyway. It may have represented a spirit helper, one of those beings that inhabited the bush that could be called on for help with the tribulations in one's life, or with troubles in the community. It might have had something to do with nox'nox, the supernatural power that is evoked from time to time by the halaits, the shamanic priests of Gitksan society. Archeologists call these things arborographs.

Whatever it was, it wasn't going to leave the Kispiox Valley, and Geel, a well-known Gitksan carver and artist, thought about ways he could take care of it, and what might be an appropriate symbol to take its place. Maybe a stone marker. Maybe a pole.

We were still talking about it hours later, back at the Suskwa roadblock camp, when old Jeff Harris from Kispiox, the 78-year-old chief Luus, showed up at the campfire and announced, "I thought we would sing together and have a little prayer."

He stood close to the fire in the afternoon sun and strapped on his banjo. This was the man who used to play in the Kispiox kazoo band, the man who stopped playing that night more than 40 years ago in the Hazelton Hall when they wouldn't let the Indians in to dance, and agreed to keep playing only after they finally did let the Indians in.

Luus handed out his hymn books. He'd been thinking a lot lately about the roadblocks, and how soon, unless the logging was slowed down, the clearcuts would be near his own house territory on the far side of Dead Horse Creek, near the old village of Kuldoe. And he'd been having bad dreams.

In one dream he was a younger man again. He was skating, and he met Sgenna and some others, and when he came back to the point on the ice where he began he found that all around him the ice was melting. There was the sound of a waterfall somewhere, and he fell through the ice, and the rushing water was pulling him down.

"Ladies and gentlemen we're here to cheer you up, you who are here blockading the road," he said. Around the fire stood Sgenna and Yagosip, Bev Anderson (now Maht, a new chief since Elsie Morrison's feast), Sabamgoss, Djogaslee, Axtiizeex, 'Noola and others. "I was very happy when Art asked me to come today. And I'm very happy to be here with you today. And you might want to know what we're planning up there in Kispiox. Tell them, Art."

Art Wilson, Wii Muugalsxw, shuffled his feet and began to speak, slow and shy, the way he is, first in Gitksan, then in English. "We still have to iron out what we're going to do, but we are talking about a blockade. We did the one-day thing a couple of years ago, and now I think the time is right. There are people suffering the elements in different places, and until we do something there, we're not going to feel much better. I think stopping traffic on the Kispiox road will go a long ways."

Everyone was quiet. The Suskwa people had met the provincial government's delegate only the day before and it had not been particularly pleasant. If anyone felt like they were standing alone on this roadblock, the news was reassuring. Yagosip smiled, then Sgenna, then 'Noola.

"Number 52," Luus called out. "I Will Bless Thee O Lord."

Everyone sang, but quietly, self-consciously. Then Number 46, Surely Goodness and Mercy, then Be Still and Know That I Am God, and In Thee O Lord I Put My Trust.

"I believe there are quite a few roadblocks all over now," Luus said between hymns. "And we have to be asking God to stop the logging." Then he sang Great Is The Lord. "Great is the Lord and greatly to be praised, In the city of our God."

Hours later, after dinner at Maht's house at Two Mile, it became evident that whatever might be said, in the disrespectful way things are usually said about the harbouring of "superstitious" beliefs, what was happening here in the City of Our God was a bit unnerving. The body of Gitwangak fireweed elder Harry Daniels was at Art Loring's house as his family made preparations for his death feast. Annabelle Fowler, Mabel White's granddaughter, had just been killed in Terrace. The telephone rang, and the word was that last night a white girl, Michelle Cummins, a waitress at the Inlander Hotel and a 21-year-old former Miss Hazelton, had just been murdered here in town.

If there is one thing I had come to learn about Gitksan country, it was something I had learned years earlier, and that is that there is meaning in everything that occurs. Whether it is the discovery of an image painted in a tree 200 years earlier, or a strange dream, or the death of a chief or a friend, nothing happens by mistake. There is a balance in nature, and there is always a sense that what happens in this world is somehow reflected by events in the spirit world, and that there are connections between those events. The natural order demands a reaction to an action. So something had happened, or something was happening, or something was about to happen.

The old worldview, and the ceremonials, devotions and

religious pursuits that went along with it, was in no way abandoned by Gitksan or Wet'suwet'en society with the coming of Christian missionaries, no matter how affectionately some people embraced Christianity. And in these mountains there was a wide range of Christianity to embrace. As in so many things, Dimlahamid is always in the centre of something, or at the edge of it, just as now it is at Dimlahamid that the Church of Mary Magdalene, with its spire rising above the houses of Hagwilget, marks the western boundary of the Roman Catholic church's Canadian province at the Wet'suwet'ens' western frontier. And it is here, where the Gitksan people live, that the coastwide domain of the Protestant churches begins.

By 1900, most Gitksan and Wet'suwet'en were at least nominally Christian, and certain villages, such as Glen Vowell and Andimaul, were established by Gitksan converts to Christianity. The Indian Affairs department's religious headcount shows that by the year 1900, there were only thirteen "pagans" left in Kispiox, where Luus comes from, but there were already 213 Methodists. At Hazelton there were 233 Anglicans and eight pagans, at Gitwangak, 144 Anglicans and five pagans, at Kisgegas, 208 Anglicans and 54 pagans, at Kitwancool, 59 Anglicans, seven pagans. The Gitksan communities were sadly divided by the new faith brought to them by the Anglican Church, the Methodists and the Salvation Army. But the church was not all bad. Whatever their spiritual contributions, the Methodists were valuable in supporting the Gitksans' land struggles. The Anglicans were also to prove helpful in the land claim struggles to come. There had even been Salvation Army officers in their uniforms at Elsie's death feast a few nights back.

Good and bad, Christian and pagan are lines that fade at the best of times, as the Salvation Army discovered to its surprise at Gitsegukla in 1897, when the alleged cannibal society adherent who ran naked, chanting dog-eater cries through a party of Indian Salvation Army members, turned out to be none other than Peter Mark, captain of the local Salvationists. A few years later, George T. Emons scrawled in his field notes that the old religion was still deeply rooted in the Gitksan, particularly at Gitwangak and Kispiox, where a "very intelligent man living under civilized conditions" in 1915 gave up waiting for white doctors to cure his consumption-ridden daughter, so he took the girl to a halait like all the other, less "civilized" Kispiox people. Emons doesn't say how the girl made out.

And it's not all that clear which came first, Christianity or the Church. The first white men to visit the Wet'suwet'en found a people who made the sign of the cross and believed in a God who had once sent his child to walk among them. Oblate father James Patrick McGucken was the first white missionary among the Wet'suwet'en, and when he arrived in 1870, the people at Moricetown and Hagwilget told him they had been expecting him for quite a while, that his arrival had been prophesied by one of their shamans who had visited heaven.

It may have started with two Indians from the Columbia River who spent years among the Red River Métis and returned to the coast in the early 1800s with a new religion influenced to some extent by Christianity. But like all new goods and ideas introduced anywhere throughout the North Pacific coast, it spread everywhere quickly. In Wet'suwet'en country, McGucken had been preceded by a prophet cult that began with Uzakli, a Babine chief, and continued through a succession of prophets, each of whom is remembered for miraculous powers. The succession concluded with Bini, who appears to have died around the time McGucken arrived at Hagwilget in 1870.

Uzakli had acquired what the Wet'suwet'en call the medicine-dream sickness, and when he recovered from it he declared that he had been to the sky where he visited with God, who gave him powers to heal the sick. Uzakli gave his followers tin crosses and sang a hymn about an angel, and the hymn proclaims him as the rope that holds up the earth. Then there was Senesaiyea, a shaman from Fraser Lake, who regularly visited heaven and is remembered for his powers to shake a rattle and cause salmon to return up rivers at an appointed time. Then came Bopa, who died, and after three days rose again with stories of an adventure to the sea, where she came to a great city where the people gave her apples. She lived another twenty years and predicted the coming of white people, who she said were really long-dead relatives of the people, and their arrival would be their return from the land of ghosts. Another Fraser Lake woman, Kokskan, followed Bopa in the succession, and she is also said to have died and come back to life. Kokskan said she did not go to the city of the dead, but went to heaven instead, where Sa (the Wet'suwet'en name for God) and his son told her to admonish her people against murder, theft and bad language. She predicted the coming of horses and cattle. It was Kokskan who taught the people the sign of the cross, and a hymn that they sang with uplifted arms, "Sa's child took and carried me aloft." She also heard confessions. Then came Lexs, who came back from heaven with a new name, Sisteyel. He was very poor, and the people didn't take him very seriously, but he had a younger brother the people did take seriously, and his name was Bini.

Bini was the greatest of all the prophets, and his miracles and teachings swept the northwest, from the Carrier to the Tsimshian. There are hundreds of spectacular and often conflicting stories about Bini the prophet, but about Bini the man, the story is that he was born Sami, given the clan name Mat, and he began his religious life when he was out with a hunting party at Decker Lake. One spring night, he lay down and mysteriously disappeared. His fellow hunters searched the camp for him, and one of the dogs finally came across him buried in the ground with only his arm protruding. Bini is known as the composer of many hymns, and he seems to have spent his fifteen-year crusade wandering the countryside and healing the sick. One of his curing methods was to ritually drink the sickness of the patient, from water in a pan. During one curing, at Fort Babine, he fell sick and died. Some suspect to this day he was poisoned. When word spread of his death, a great assembly of his followers carried him in a great procession to the Bulkley River. He is buried at Hagwilget, in the ground below Joey Pierre's crucifix.

People rarely seem to die alone in this country. One death seems to follow upon another, and when it happens there is a mood in the reserves of anticipation, and people look for meaning in what outsiders might consider merely an unfortunate sequence of tragedies. It is not a dread, exactly, but an unease, a vague awareness that something is moving through the countryside. It was like that in 1862, when the people looked up to see the sun disappearing. What followed the solar eclipse of that year was a mood of fear, because the people believed a great pestilence followed such occurrences. And people started getting sick and dying. At Hagwilget, the most powerful of the shamans was Yip, who could see the sickness moving through the air, and he tried to catch it in a salmon basket but his medicine was not powerful enough. Before the year had passed, hundreds of Gitksan and Wet'suwet'en had died during what was to be remembered as the smallpox epidemic of 1862.

In 1989, the mood of unease was not helped by the tension over the roadblocks, the angry words in the South Town bar, the people on the reserves waiting for Victoria to act against them or wondering whether some of the loggers would get drunk in New Town and head out to the road-block looking for trouble some night. It was hard to define, but the mood was unsettled.

It was that way when Adam Gagnon unearthed the ochre-covered grave over in Moricetown in 1987, the day the land claims trial opened in Vancouver. In the ten days before Gagnon's backhoe started turning up bits of bone that September morning, four elders died, and there was feasting and mourning throughout the Skeena Valley. First it was Agnes Sutton, a matriarch of the frog clan, who died at the age of 97. Then Thomas Wright, an 86-year-old wolf clan chief from Gitanmaax. Then it was 86-year-old Martha Brown, a much-loved wolf clan elder from Kispiox, and then Christine Wesley, also 86, a fireweed elder from Gitsegukla. All in ten days.

"I don't know what it is," Maht said. The kitchen was warm and quiet, and outside the window nothing much moved on the dark roads through Two Mile, that half-way community between Old Town and New Town. She sat with her broth-er Luu Goom'kw and her husband of ten years, Ian. When these things happen, these deaths, the talk inevitably turns to the haldowgets, and when the subject of recovery comes up, the talk turns to the halaits. The halaits and the haldowgets are organized into two secret societies, each of which maintains ritual privilege and supernatural power. The halaits are heal-ers and are respected in the community. The haldowgets are more inclined to inflict injury, and are feared. Few outsiders, anthropologists or otherwise, have been able to assemble much information about them. Their identities are a secret, and nobody likes to talk about them, at least publicly or for the record, but there's often hushed-voice speculation about who might be a haldowget, or who saw so-and-so hiding in a ditch in his regalia, or who said so-and-so is a halait.

Maht is a fireweed chief now, and her mind is preoccupied with her new responsibilities. A 44-year-old public health nurse who grew up one of eleven children on a farm in the Kispiox Valley, Maht is well respected in the community. She is one of a growing number of chiefs whose priority is the abandonment of the reserves and a return to the land. She sees an evil in the reserves, the ugliness bred by confinement and welfare and alcoholism, and she holds that the community's greatest social problems may well arise from the decline of the halaits and the five "natural doctors," exercise, fresh air, nutrition, water and rest. The haldowgets, meanwhile, are coming to be identified with the syndrome of despair and self-destruction that prevails on the reserves.

The roles played by the halaits, the haldowgets and the powers upon which they draw, in the interplay between Gitksan culture and the colonial authority, may never be fully understood, or at least documented, by outsiders. Despite their decline, the halaits are still present in Gitksan society, and they are active in the "land-claim," not only in the struggle on the ground in Gitksan country, but even so many hundreds of miles away as Courtroom 53 of that glass and concrete structure on Robson Street in the centre of downtown Vancouver. As Mas Gak explained one night at the roadblock camp, the halaits had been exerting influence on the various players in the court case all along, even Judge McEachern. The halaits were particularly interested in McEachern, "working on him," and advising Mas Gak when he was most receptive to influence. They had been "working on him" at certain times of the day and certain times of the night when he was asleep. There were halaits, he said, with power to "communicate" with him, sometimes by talking to him in his sleep, and sometimes with ceremonies involving the use of candles, herbs and medicines. The halaits had also been an unseen presence, a year before the Suskwa blockade, during the protracted roadblock campaign to halt Westar's construction of a logging road and bridge across the Babine River at Sam Green Creek. In the early weeks of the Babine roadblocks the halaits were having dreams that something would happen, and their dreams were about the catskinner working for Westar Timber, Doug Hamblin, the lead tractor operator clearing the right-of-way through the bush towards the camp at the river's edge.

A few weeks before that September morning, Mas Gak's nephew, Andy Clifton, went out to warn Hamblin about the medicine he was toying with. A few days later the tractor rolled, but Hamblin was unhurt. Westar officials came in by helicopter to assess the damage, and the work was moved to an area further back along the road. This time, Hamblin was at the controls of a backhoe, and the backhoe tipped on him. Mas Gak described the area as a place where the nox'nox were known to be present and active. So Hamblin was again warned to leave. In the weeks after the September standoff when Luu Goom'kw and Wii Seeks took their stand, Doug Hamblin was working in the next valley, and in an accident of some sort he was killed when a tree fell on him.

However effective the nox'nox, the halaits and the haldowgets may be, they certainly seem to turn up as either minor characters or key players throughout the conflict that has evolved into the current standoff known as *Delgamuukw versus The Queen*.

In 1872, during the Gitksans' first blockade — the blockade of the Skeena River that was precipitated by the "accidental" burning of Gitksegukla — halaits perform key roles in the opening scene. The fire began during the salmon fishery, and the village was empty except for the wife of the chief Skogumlaxha and three halaits who stayed behind to look after her. The halaits were engaged in their work at Wilp Yip (House of Earth), so called because it was built into the side of a hill and was soundproof. The senior halait, a man named Wen, emerged from Wilp Yip to find the village burning.

In the state of seige that occurred in 1887 and was to become known as the Skeena River Rebellion, a haldowget plays a central role. The haldowget was a man named Neetuh, and he was executed in retribution for sickness and death that had swept through the Gitksan territories. It was Neetuh's execution that set off the chain of events that led to the so-called rebellion.

From the scant written record, the story begins with a measles epidemic that was killing people in Gitanmaax. The chiefs there were enraged, attributing the epidemic to the few white settlers in the country, and the settlers sought refuge behind the meagre palisades of the Hudson's Bay Company post at Hazelton.

For the Gitksan, the real story begins a little earlier than that. From a peculiar piece of work, a sort of non-fiction novel called *The Downfall of Temlaham* written by the famous anthropologist Marius Barbeau and first published in 1928, and from the Gitksan traditions of the so-called rebellion, the story begins with Sunbeams.

A key fireweed chief in the Skeena Valley at the time, Sunbeams of Gitsegukla saw that other hands were at work in the plague, those of Neetuh, her uncle. Neetuh, whose name means Looking At His Reflection In The Water, had ambitions for the chieftanship of Hanamuk, to which one of Sunbeams' sons, Gamahaum (Bitten-Wrists — a name with origins in the ada'ox of the Medeek, the great bear spirit that laid waste to Dimlahamid) was entitled. The holder of the name Hanamuk would possess large tracts of productive land and would command much respect throughout the Gitksan and Wet'suwet'en confederacy, so the ascendancy was much prized. Largely through Sunbeams' forceful diplomacy and palace intrigue among the clans and houses, a rough campaign even by Gitksan standards, Neetuh's pretensions had failed along with his sorcery, and Gamahaum was inducted into the name Hanamuk, much to Neetuh's anger.

Sunbeams' husband and Gamahaum's father was a man by the name of Kamalmuk, a wolf clan member of rank, known to the fur traders as Kitwancool Jim, a "Christianized Indian" who had spent years with white mining prospectors and who wasn't much partial to traditional politics. If in nothing else, he was united with his wife in grief, with the death by measles in 1887 of their son Gamahaum and their younger son, Kumas. Elsewhere along Skeena, Bulkley, Kispiox and Babine rivers, Gitskan and Wet'suwet'en people were dying from the measles in dozens, and a powerful chief at Gitanmaax, Gyetm Guldoo, lost three daughters. Gyetm Guldoo — whose name in 1989 was held by Sylvester Green, one of the chiefs leading the Suskwa Valley blockade — urged the execution of all the whites in the countryside in retaliation, knowing that they brought the disease and suspecting that it was spread deliberately in the sugar that the Hudson's Bay trader at Hazelton had distributed so liberally all summer. But to Sunbeams, the tragedy demanded a more substantial remedy, and punishing the white people would not suffice. It was Neetuh the haldowget who had cursed her son. A debt must be paid, and balance had to be restored. Kamalmuk didn't need much convincing, either. To restore order, Neetuh would have to be punished.

On a snow-covered bluff on the trail about four miles below Kitwancool, at a place known as Wendzel-neleetu, Kamalmuk took aim with his old flintlock and fired at Neetuh below. It was a fairly clean hit, but it still took Neetuh two days to die. He had crawled into a tangle of roots under a wind-downed tree.

The killing precipitated an interesting challenge under

Gitksan law. It wasn't the run-of-the-mill kind of crime. The remedy would clearly have to provide a greater and more secure balance of justice than the eye-for-an-eye dictum that normally obtained among the Gitksan in such circumstances. Here we had a wolf, husband to a fireweed of great nobility, who had killed a fireweed haldowget in retribution for the death of his sons, both fireweeds. And the fireweeds had a problem: among many there was a natural predisposition in favour of Kamalmuk's actions, but Neetuh, in death, still had many supporters in his camp, and there was no clear evidence that his execution had just cause. Certainly the powerful Gyetm Guldoo didn't think so.

After much consultation among the ranking chiefs, the matter was adroitly resolved. Settlement involved a feast to redress the grievance, at which the wolves, Kamalmuk's people, pledged two of Kamalmuk's brothers as slaves to Kwawmats, Neetuh's successor in the fireweeds, and they would see to his every comfort. Kamalmuk was to fast in silence for four days. Justice had been done and the matter was settled to everyone's satisfaction.

Unfortunately, the matter didn't end there. With the whites cowering unnecessarily behind jerry-built earthworks at Hazelton and a strange-looking tower constructed from raw logs to serve as a sort of defensive bastion in the event of an attack, the provincial authorities in Victoria were alerted to the situation on the far-off Skeena. But the whites were afraid because the natives were afraid, and the natives were afraid because one P. Washburn, a sometime-prospector and meddler in local affairs, had announced high and low that he was off to Victoria to ensure that British law, not Gitksan law, would prevail in the circumstances of Neetuh's death.

The Gitksans were well aware where that sort of attitude might lead. Only fifteen years earlier, the gunboats had arrived at the mouth of the Skeena after the Gitsegukla chiefs blockaded the river in response to the burning of their village by white prospectors.

So in 1887, the scene in the Skeena was tense, so much so that in a tragic misunderstanding a madman by the name of Tupesuh at Gitsegukla shot at what he thought was an attacker, and in return fire, the madman was killed. Apart from that, nothing much in the way of rebellion took place in 1887. At the white settlement at Hazelton, while loyal subjects throughout the British Empire celebrated Queen Victoria's Golden Jubilee, fearful settlers peered out over the newly constructed ramparts imagining armies of angry red men. But there wasn't an Indian to be seen.

Then, in the spring of 1888, the HMS *Caroline*, a British gunboat, dropped anchor at the mouth of the Skeena. A posse of special constables headed upriver. Kamalmuk, "Kitwancool Jim," had resigned himself to surrender, to deal with British law and get it over with. But at the last moment, when he was confronted by two police constables early one morning at the house of Nee-ranyah in Gitwangak, where he was staying, for some reason he ran. The police had instructions only to locate him, but Kamalmuk was shot in the back by a special police constable, one Billy Green.

Green found himself incarcerated the next day in Hazelton along with Gitsegukla chief Mawlahan and another Gitsegukla native whose name was reported as unpronounceable. The Gitsegukla pair were held in connection with the death of the madman Tupesuh. When it was all over, all three were acquitted, Green for Kamalmuk's murder and the two Gitsegukla noblemen for the accidental death of a madman. The whole incident, precipitated by Victoria's reaction to the application of Gitksan law in a haldowget's execution, left relations between the Gitksan chiefs and Victoria in tatters, and a tragic imbalance remained unattended in Gitksan law that colonial law could not set to rights.

Whatever it was that was moving through this countryside in 1989 obviously had something to do with contemporary forest-clearcutting technology, but it was not just Westar Timber or Skeena Cellulose and it involved something older and more malevolent than what appears on forest ministry charts and in allowable-annual-cut regulations. Whatever it was, its impact is felt deepest in the poverty of the reserves the government surveyors laid out over the protests of the chiefs wherever they went.

"That's why it's so important to get back out on the land," Maht said, pouring another cup of tea. "That's the basic premise with the halaits. To look after the physical aspect of your body. And then there's a whole other side, spirituality, meditation. I think what we all really have to do is get back out on the land."

Which is just what her brother Luu Goom'kw decided to do about eight years earlier. Sitting with his arms crossed, leaning away from the table on the two hind legs of his chair, the 36-year-old carver and painter said he felt a little bit embarrassed to talk about it, but there was a time, after he turned his back on reserve life, when he actually learned how to talk to trees.

"How it started," he said, "was that I thought this rat race could do with one less rat. I just wanted the peace and freedom. It was about 1982. The timing was right, I think. I was 28 years old, full of piss and vinegar, like I could conquer the world, do anything I wanted to do.

"It was in the Kuldoe area," he explained.

Kuldoe, about 60 miles up the Skeena River from Two Mile on an old trapline trail, is still beyond the reach of logging roads and clearcuts. It's a quiet place, an ancient village site at the base of a mountainside, and there's not much there but gravehouses and the remains of old community houses. The totem poles were cut down and floated out of there by museum curators years ago.

"I have to tell a little bit of a story. My uncle Pete said, 'Go out there. Live out there. Talk to the trees.' So I did. But they don't talk back. They just stood there. I was just, I don't know, doing it. Nothing happened. But then after one sixteen-hour day, I was just beat, and I stopped in my snow-shoe tracks and lay down and they said, 'Oh, you poor thing.' I looked up. Well, it was a lot easier to go that last four miles to the cabin.

"The first year wasn't a very good year. I was even look-ing at the crows and thinking how good they'd look in the stew pot, and I was drumming a tune on my ribs because I was so skinny. By the next year, holy ... I had lots of food. Trout, moose, deer, grouse. I remember thinking that once you learn how, it's really cheap. There were times when I would feel like singing out at the top of my voice out there. I don't think I ever feel so good as when I'm out there."

Maht and Ian would go out to stay with him from time to time. Maht remembers they lived well off the fruits of the land, salmon and berries and something called ax, a fern root that tastes like sweet potato and grows in bunches like tiny bananas. "I'd feel so safe out there," Bev said, "even if we heard wolves or saw grizzly bears or grizzly tracks, it was safe. It was so safe."

Said Ian: "You become stronger, the winds, the snow, all those things you're up against. You're healthier for it."

And you're away from everything, Maht said. "It's like a fair here. When you're out of the bush, all the people are try-ing to sell you something. You've got to have a video or a four-wheel-drive or something. That's what life outside the land is like. On the reserves, I see child sexual abuse, wife abuse, and pain, really, really bad psychic pain. And no encouragement at all. I make it a point to try and be encouraging to people. They need to be more loving and caring to one another."

Luu Goom'kw answers the telephone, a call from Art Loring's house. It was about the death feast for Harry Daniels. He hung up, and after he talked it over with Maht and Ian, it was decided: there was no way the Kispiox roadblock could go ahead just yet. What with Daniels being another death among the fireweeds, the clan would be all but broke if this kept up. There were too many feast preparations to be looked after, and the Kispiox roadblock meeting that Wii Muugalsxw talked about that afternoon would have to be put off a day or two.

Late that night back at the Suskwa camp it was quiet. There were no chiefs, there was no Luus, no Nearer My God To Thee. It had been about three weeks since the Suskwa roadblock first went up, and tomorrow in the government offices in Victoria and in the law offices and forest company headquarters in Vancouver the talk would be about Denhoff's weekend visit here with the chiefs, about how he had returned south without convincing anybody to take the roadblock down. Indian Affairs Minister Pierre Cadieux would soon be on his way to Victoria to talk with B.C.'s politicians about the province's Indian troubles. The talk around the campfire, what there was of it, was still about the deaths of Harry Daniels, Annabelle Fowler and Michelle Cummins, all in the past three days, and about the upcoming feasts. Then there was that sentry figure, or the spirit helper, or whatever it was, that Geel and his family had taken back from the high country above the Kispiox Valley that morning. Haa'txw, carving a piece of wood and warming himself by the fire against the cold night air, said the image that had stared out of the hemlock tree in that lonely and distant place for so many generations might be any number of things, that there are many things that move through the forests that people don't know much about.

There is the giant lynx, there are frogs that kill with invisible distance weaponry, huge snake monsters and little hairy men, and none of the churches had banished them from this bush. In the 1920s an old Wet'suwet'en told anthropologist Diamond Jenness: "Today, the priests say we lie, but we know better. The white man has been only a short time in this country and knows very little about the animals. We have lived here thousands of years and we were taught long ago by the animals themselves."

There are animals that can take possession of human souls, Haa'txw said, cutting another sliver from the wood piece he was carving. These animals are called 'Watsx. If you are being haunted, he explained, you can say, "That must be the 'Watsx," and their power over you is broken.

'Noola sat down at the fire beside Haa'txw, pushed the soot-covered tea kettle closer to the embers and talked about another thing that is known to move through the countryside from time to time. It is the Waadimxw, a woman that roams the bush from the coast far inland, and although she is described as a myth, 'Noola said, she was sighted less than two years ago. Mel Woods and Howard Sexsmith were there when she was seen, but she ran off into the bush and disappeared.

"You hear her baby crying," 'Noola said. "She carries it on her back. She has long hair, with really long fingernails, and the baby's got the same thing. If you can come up behind her, and take her baby and hold it out, you can ask her for good luck for all your family, and when she gives you something tangible, cedar bark, I think it is, then you give the baby back to her."

Then there is the small man. Soup Wilson's mother was picking soapberries when she saw the small man. He is covered in hair. They ran away from the place they saw the man and left everything behind.

'Noola told a story of his grandfather, sleeping alone in one of the old houses out in the bush. He heard the sound of old women's voices, old women laughing, and moving through the bush towards the house. "He said, 'That would be the 'Watsx,' and the laughing stopped right away. It just stopped right away."

The 'Watsx, 'Noola explained, is something like a river otter with powers to become man-like. And I remembered from years earlier having heard about this animal. It had something to do with transformation, a theme that pops up in religions from coastal Siberia to North America's northwest coast. The 'Watsx has a special relationship with the dead, and stories of its occurrence sometimes emerge in stories about drowning. The 'Watsx has something to do with death and madness.

Among the Wet'suwet'en are the remnants of a religious order, the Kyanyuantan, with priestly functions specific to the control of kyan, the power of animal spirits to possess the soul. The most malevolent of those spirits was the otter spirit, the spirit the Gitksan called 'Watsx. Its victims, Jenness observed, exhibited violent hysteria, dementia and a craving for human flesh. Kyanyuantan initiates were drawn from kyan victims who had been possessed themselves but had been trained to control the spirit by members of the religious order. Untreated, the victim dies. Jenness attended an exhausting two-hour healing ceremony at the home of Old Sam at Hagwilget in 1924, conducted by three women, themselves victims but in control of the incubus. The ceremony was for Old Sam's wife, whose possession began with recurring dreams about the otter. After the ritual, the normally skeptical Jenness concluded that "clearly the morbid condition of each woman was neither fictitious nor consciously self-induced."

Years ago there was a woman, 'Noola explained, who was possessed by the 'Watsx. "These people tried to catch her, and they went to a place where the 'Watsx was, after they eventually caught her. You take the bladder of the 'Watsx, the otter, the one that is the mate of the woman, and then you mix it with Indian hellebore, and smear it on the woman. Gradually, the woman will come to."

In his submission on the Wet'suwet'en people to the Bureau of American Ethnology, Jenness noted four cases of kyan possession reported to him at Hagwilget that had gone untreated between 1915 and 1925. In the first two cases, Old Sam explained to him, the priest at the recently constructed Church of Mary Magdalene convinced the Kyanyuantan to leave the victims alone, and the victims died. In the next two cases, both the priest and the local doctor sent the victims to the Essondale mental institution outside of Vancouver. Within months, they also died.

"There was another woman," 'Noola went on, "and she's dead now and I don't think I should mention her name. She was a very well-kept woman, and then she just stopped combing her hair. She eventually drank herself to death. She would say" — and 'Noola spoke first in Gitksan, then in English — " 'That bad thing, the naughty thing. It was furry.' She died about ten years ago."

My muscles were still stiff from pulling the sentry figure tree through the deep undergrowth that morning, and we were all dead tired. The rain was falling in waves. We could hear it falling in the trees a short distance off, and the rushing hiss of it, like the sound of old women's voices, would move slowly through the dark until the hard rain clattered on the tarpaulin covering the kitchen camp.

"That must be the 'Watsx," Haa'txw said. He was quiet a moment, then he laughed out loud at his joke. It was late, and the fire was dying.

THE BLUEJAY
ALIGHTS AT
GITWANGAK

When the end came, the gatehouse was in flames. It was late at night. Sgenna went for his rifle, figuring he should be able to get at least one good shot in. He figured it should go just above the midway point between the tail lights that were disappearing into the dark, heading north into the no-go area behind the Suskwa roadblock.

Sgenna and Yagosip had come to check in at the Suskwa camp. It was a visit to see what needed doing, to see that everybody was alright and that there hadn't been any trouble. They had seen the flames from back along the road that coiled down from Highway 16, and they saw that it was the gatehouse well before their pickup crossed the Bulkley River bridge.

It had been an interesting few days.

After the initial delays over Elsie Morrison's feast and the news of Harry Daniels' death, the chiefs with house territories in the Kispiox Valley finally met to talk about a new roadblock to stop timber coming out of the Kispiox timber supply area. Sitting at tables at the community hall under the updrawn basketball hoops and the Welcome To Kispiox banner were Wii Seeks, Gordon Sebastian, Sgenna and Yagosip, Luu Goom'kw, Wii Muugalsxw, Delgamuukw, Antiigililbix, Yaya, Axtiizeex, Maht and Ian, Luus, Daakhluumgyet, Kenny Rabnett and David Silver and a few others. There was another group about as big in the glassed-in anteroom upstairs, busy with Monday night bingo. Luus opened the roadblock meeting with a prayer.

"We ask thee, Lord, for your mercy, and that you guide all those who came to this meeting, and that you protect them in Jesus' name," Luus prayed. "And that the next time we hold the road, we'll hold it for good."

The first item of discussion was the news about what had happened on Vancouver Island, where some loggers had successfully sued a handful of protesters, the Friends of Clayoquot Sound, who had built treehouses and moored their boats below a road blasting site to stop a logging operation that was cutting through some of the last old-growth timber on the west coast. So it was up to Gordon, since he was a lawyer, to explain what it might mean.

To begin with, he said, you're Indians, and for another thing you're Gitksan and you own the place. But for another thing, if he went trapping in Axtiizeex's territory without getting permission there would be a real hullabaloo, but if he went in there as a logger working for a big logging outfit nobody would say anything.

"I don't understand that," Gordon said. "You think the court case itself is going to somehow give us title to the land. It's not like that. You ask if we could get sued. Well, that's a good question, but it's not likely they're going to get anything for loss of wages. But if they do sue, where are they going to get the money from us? Even if they do sue, how are they going to get us to pay?"

Gordon had been running on empty for a while now. He didn't like to give speeches and he didn't like to take things too seriously. So at first, he didn't say anything much. As usual, he let other people speak. And they talked about how many millions of dollars in timber was leaving their house territories and how a roadblock was long overdue, but then again there are the death feasts to consider, and maybe it would be best to leave the whole thing alone for a while. Then again, they'd already talked at two other meetings about going ahead with another blockade on the Kispiox Road, so maybe it was time for a decision. They talked about how good it was when Luus came out to the Suskwa to sing hymns and lift everyone's spirits. Somebody said that the Kitwancool chiefs were waiting to see what was going to happen here before going ahead with plans for a blockade over on their end. And maybe there should be a meeting with the loggers first, to explain things, and after all the land claim was for them, too, so their children could have jobs, and how important it was for the Gitksan chiefs to stand together in these things. Gordon listened, and he listened some more, and then it came his turn to speak.

It's fine to talk about shutting everything down, he said, but the fact is that most of the millworkers are from the villages, and if it's support you're talking about you're going to have to deal with them. The men without jobs are waiting for work, like work is maybe just going to appear like a nice surprise sometime, somewhere. Like Hagwilget. The band trained 49 people for various jobs, and only 27 of them are working, Gordon said. And there are 100 more employable adults on welfare, too.

Everybody listened. Gordon didn't speak much at these things.

"You know, I see our people on reserve. A good 90 per cent of the people, a good 90 per cent. They're poor."

It was like he needed to get something off his chest.

"They're very poor. And you know, I live off the backs of the poor people. I'm on the band council. I have a job because of those poor people on the reserve.

"Sunday morning when I went to the Suskwa roadblock? There was nobody there. So I went over to the road and put up the block. I put up the blockade. No problem. One little Indian. One little Hagwilget Indian, for a couple of hours. Don't you see how strong you are? I didn't have 200 Indians there. There was just one. And you know who's been manning that roadblock? You know who's manning that roadblock now? Poor people. It's the poor people. They're living off grouse and moose meat, and whatever food we bring out. Poor people."

Everybody was quiet. It was true that most mornings that I stumbled out of my tent in the bush camp, the people there were 'Noola, Soup, Josh and Haa'txw. They were the ones who took turns at the blockade, moving the wood blocks for local residents and handing out the fishing permits and asking for the ten dollars per permit. They were the ones who would sometimes have to take a deep breath, try to look tough and turn white people away. 'Noola, who'd grown up in a little house on the outskirts of Gitanmaax with eight brothers and two sisters and hadn't had a real job in years. Soup and Josh, who had their vertebrae crushed and their legs smashed in the forest industry, and the thinning jobs they'd had they lost when the chiefs decided to shut down the Suskwa. And Haa'txw, who'd spent almost half his life roaming the countryside looking for work, and much of that time as a California farmworker, and now he was living at the Suskwa bush camp because he didn't really have any other home to call his own.

"And then there is the plan. Who do we want to plan for? For the white man, when he asks us what the plan is? A plan to include the white people? If we plan to include the white people, we have to be strong. Well, look around this table. It would take us half an hour to develop a good plan for a cutting block. We don't need an excuse. If it's an excuse we need, we're not doing our job."

It took a minute or two for everybody to think about that, but then things were underway. Gordon was right, Wii Seeks said. There weren't even many people at this meeting, but that's alright, too.

"People aren't here tonight because the agenda is too hard," Wii Seeks said. "The decision is too difficult. So that leaves us to do what we know is right. We have no choice, even if we are just a few. There will always be people who oppose what we do. That element will always be there. The important thing is that we do what's right. We must demonstrate our own authority. Nobody is going to give it to us. We must take it."

Everybody had their say after that, and everybody was in agreement. A blockade it would be. Wii Muugalsxw was happy. This was like those days in February the year before, only this time the roadblock wasn't going to come down by mistake.

So Wii Muugalsxw went to work on a huge sheet of paper he'd taped to the wall with headings and categories listed at the top. Everybody called out to fill in the blanks. Under "Camp Policy" went "No" and the list: violence booze drugs sex badmouthing. Under "Obstruction" went gate gravel log (for now), "Outside Support" elicited Gitwangak Eagles Kitwancool United Church Stein. The sheet of paper filled quickly.

"Who says Sunday?" Wii Muugalsxw asked. Everybody's hands went up. "Then it's Sunday."

That left six days to plan, and there was a lot going on in between to make things more interesting, particularly that big meeting the chiefs and the woodworkers' union leaders had agreed to pull together for the following night at Gitwangak.

It was bigger than anyone expected. About 120 people showed up, and the chiefs were there with a feast. There was salmon and bannock and rice and potatoes and bread and apples and oranges. There was Keith Spencer from Westar Timber, Surinder Malhotra from the IWA, the truck loggers, the logging contractors, the millworkers and the townspeople. It was something that had never really happened before. There were white people and Indian people sitting together, eating together and talking together about the land where they lived as neighbours.

What had brought them together was the prospect of a complete fracture in the local economy. Westar needed 1.2 million cubic metres of wood every year to feed sawlogs through its mills at Gitwangak and Carnaby, but it had licences to cut only 717,000 cubic metres, and half of that ended up good for nothing but pulp. Stege Logging needed 250,000 cubic metres of wood but all it had a licence to take in the area was 64,000 cubic metres. Kitwanga Lumber had a licence to cut 77,000 cubic metres of timber in the region every year, but its mill needed 200,000 to stay at full bore. Most of the decent wood had already been cut. The wood the mills were cutting now was half Hemlock Surprise. The mills were staying alive by buying logs from private lands and from small business licences and by importing wood from elsewhere in the province. The forest base in the chiefs' territories was already vastly overcommitted as it was, but as if to rub salt in their wounds the B.C. government had only two days earlier stitched together another sale of wood from the same overcut forests. A Prince Rupert mill needed some pulpwood, so the forests ministry was offering an annual take of 623,000 cubic metres of wood, over and above the annual allowable cut, every year for the following 25 years. Much of that volume was proposed to come from the already-ravaged Kispiox timber supply area.

The local millworkers were watching helplessly as more than 300 fully loaded logging trucks headed out of the northern bush for the saltwater at Stewart to feed mills in Vancouver and Japan. Westar Timber had been pleading with the government to end the controversial practice of whole log exports from the Kalum and Cassiar areas, on the Gitksans' northern frontiers. But Victoria wouldn't budge. Sometimes it seemed as though the B.C. forests ministry was deliberately mining the forests to get rid of them as soon as it could. And in fact that was exactly the government's official policy, and precisely the big companies' policy: get rid of the forests, replace them with plantations. In the Kalum and Cassiar, the plan was to clear the forest to replace it with an even-aged stand of more merchantable species to be cut down again, two lifetimes down the road. The companies that first went into the Kalum and Cassiar bush country north of Kitwancool had started up operations at about the time *Delgamuukw versus The Queen* opened in Vancouver. In the three years that had passed between that day in Vancouver and this night in Gitwangak, three million cubic metres of timber, about enough wood to build a city of 200,000 people, had been dumped into the saltwater at Stewart. Some of it went to Vancouver, mostly for pulp. The rest was auctioned off to overseas markets. When the Cassiar-Kalum clearcutting plans were opened up, the main outfits — Tay-M, Buffalo Head and Orenda — offered a series of regional investments in the bids that won them their licences. There was supposed to be a log chipping plant, a sawmill, an extraction plant, a pole-peeling operation — a total of fourteen milling operations. None of them had come through. The three firms were paying a quarter of the provincial stumpage rates. The replanting programs that were supposed to be the point of all this were constantly falling apart, partly because the wages the companies paid wouldn't bring anyone in. In the fall of 1987, Tay-M's silviculture program didn't materialize because it started to rain, the mushrooms started to sprout, and all the treeplanters went picking mushrooms because there was more money in it. The loggers themselves could barely make ends meet. Bankruptcies and lawsuits left logging trucks idle. The loggers who stayed on the road freely admitted to anyone who asked that what they were involved in easily surpassed the worst logging practices they'd ever seen. From time to time, the air was dark with the smoke of piling fires — 50 to 60 truckloads of wood at a time incinerated because the trees had more than ten per cent rot in them. Logger Roland Lavoie said it was the ugliest logging operation he'd ever seen, with some burning pilings filled with wood that was at least half merchantable. Bridgebuilder Doug McIntyre reckoned that about one-third of the felled trees in the area ended up as burning pyres. Leo Cotie had been working in the bush twenty years, and he said he'd never seen anything like it, but everybody was on piece work instead of an hourly rate, so whole forests got chopped down and left on the ground to get at the fraction of merchantable timber the rest of the trees were hiding.

The Indians had been up on all this from the start. What they'd warned against was coming to pass, and it looked as though the regional forest-based economy was about to collapse on itself. In the Gitksan and Wet'suwet'en territories, the Indian roadblocks were slowly shutting down the whole countryside, blockading the forests that were left. Even IWA leaders were quietly asking them to push into the north a bit and shut down Kalum and Cassiar. Suddenly everybody seemed interested in what the Indians had to say about things.

Among the chiefs and speakers in the Gitwangak hall were Sgenna, Yagosip, Solomon Marsden, Wii Muugalsxw, Tenimgyet, Glen Williams, Gordon Sebastian, Mas Gak, Wii Seeks, Xsimwits'iin, Giila'wa, Niist and Djogaslee.

Gordon was the chairman of the meeting. Mas Gak was there in his appointed role as speaker for the chiefs, and he got into it right away.

A key element of Mas Gak's plan had been to try and convince the non-natives within the Gitksan and Wet'suwet'en territories to take a hard look around them and try to see their interests best defended in an alliance with the Indians under the chiefs' authority. If the forest industry regime in the area wasn't going to convince them, little would. The first item on Thursday night's agenda was to explain to the white people where it was they really lived, whose country it really was, what the land claim and the court case were all about and how they might like to fit in.

He began by walking the audience through the landscape, to show them what had brought the chiefs to this fork in the trail. Along the way there had been legal attempts to put new forest tenures on hold while *Delgamuukw versus The Queen* was still in the courts. Those plans had been resisted. The chiefs had made overtures to talk to the government about what they saw happening on the land around them. Those overtures were rebuffed. There were specific areas the chiefs warned the government to keep its forest licences away from. Those areas were the Gitwangak west, from Oliver Creek to Gitwangak, the Gitsegukla Valley's west side, the Mill Lake area up in the Kitwancool, the Babine forests, the Upper Skeena, the Bell-Irving corridor, the untouched Wet'suwet'en country and the Upper Suskwa. Those warnings were ignored.

Instead, the rate of clearcutting increased, and it was hard to find an Indian anywhere who wasn't convinced that Victoria's Social Credit politicians and the big forest companies that supported them knew they would lose in court so they were taking out as much wood as possible before the game was up.

So the war had to be fought in the courts, but it also had to be fought on the land. And if the white people wanted to participate with the chiefs in making the economic and political decisions that were being made in Victoria and Ottawa, then now was the time to speak up. A task force on the forest industry would be a good place to start, Mas Gak suggested.

"At this point, the chiefs and the house groups aren't interested in escalating this," said Mas Gak. "Our fight is not with you. You're just caught in the squeeze."

Around the tables, among the Gitksan and Wet'suwet'en, the logging contractors and the truckers and the white mill hands sat quietly. There was Brian Larson, Norman Larson, Martin Penner, Dave Ness, Bill Macrae and Steve Leary. There was Dan Madlung from Westar and Gary Arnold from WJ Logging. There was even Dave Webster, the new mayor of New Town. He'd taken over from Pete Weeber, the Westar woodlands manager who'd been stopped by Wii Seeks and the others that morning at Sam Green Creek. Dave Webster was the one the Kispiox chiefs were waiting for that night almost two years earlier when they'd taken down their blockade to let the loggers through, only to find that Webster and the others weren't coming. And now here he was. There were white people who normally refused to sit with Indians at the New Town bar. There were white people who wanted to feel at home and be neighbourly but couldn't because of their confusion about the land claim. And there were white people who seemed to get along with the Indians just fine in spite of it all.

"If you have something you want to say, let her fly," Gordon said, opening the floor to questions.

The job of breaking the ice fell to Keith Spencer, vice-president of Westar Timber, the fixer the company parachuted into a countryside full of restless Indians just a few weeks before the first logging road showdown during the 1988 Babine River campaign. Back then, when he was asked what he thought about the Gitksans' claims to the land, he said the whole thing was "rubbish."

Spencer wasn't talking like that anymore. He walked up to the microphone between the tables to the right of the head table on the stage, where the chiefs sat. He started off by agreeing right off the bat that whole log exports had to stop, that the uncertainty caused by the increased pressure on the local forests was intolerable, and whatever people had said or done in the past, if this was an opportunity to start something new and constructive, he was for it. It had got to the point where Westar officials were losing as much sleep about the banks as the truck loggers were losing with worry over whether they'd lose their trucks, he said. The task force the chiefs were proposing sounded like a good deal to him.

"That would be a great start, to get on top of that one. I just don't know anything else. As far as myself, personally, I have an interest in keeping the businesses running, for two reasons. The first is that I've always worked in the sawmills. I don't know how to work in anything else. Number two is I've always enjoyed working with people and I want to keep them employed. It's a difficult position ... with the issues that have come up, with the blockades that have come up, I think everybody has taken a sensible approach to it all."

Before he turned to sit down, he thought a moment. Then he said he thought it was about time the government recognized the chiefs' land claims arguments, stopped resisting them in the courts, and sat down at the bargaining table as the chiefs had asked.

The Indians clapped. The white people clapped. Spencer's

comments set the tone for the evening. Things were definitely looking up.

Gary Arnold said the time had come to talk, and after all it was his kids and the Indian kids that the whole thing was really about. Surinder Malhotra from the IWA got up and blasted the government's forest policies, its silviculture policies and its log export policies, and said the local people had to stand up for themselves, Indians and non-Indians. Brian Larson, who'd been shut down by the Suskwa roadblock, said this kind of talk was new to him, but he liked it. The "segregation bullshit" had to end, there were native Indians and native whites, and the people should be working together, and they should be equal in all things, hunting and fishing rights included. Dan Madlung said he was behind the whole proposal for co-operation, but he wasn't sure how the Gitksan system worked, who was in control, who he was supposed to talk to if he wanted to chop a tree or catch a fish or shoot a grouse. Steve Leary said it was a good thing to talk like this, the Indians and whites were neighbours, and after all he went to school with Wii Seeks and they both got bad grades, so what would it mean if the Indians won? Who would be in charge? How does it all work?

Mas Gak, Wii Seeks, Djogaslee and Marvin George took turns explaining how things work, and how things might work when the Indians won. A lot would have to be worked out in negotiations, but the key thing is the authority of the chiefs over their particular territories. People could have multiple status after the aboriginal title is confirmed by the courts, but the authority of the chiefs, as developed and sustained in the feast system, would have to be respected. This was the modern world. There were fax machines and telephones and skilled people to rely on. Nobody need be turned away.

It was a lot for people to absorb in a night's discussion at the Gitwangak community hall, but it was further than the debate had ever gone.

"There's going to be a transition period," Mas Gak explained. "We don't want to see any of these big bureaucracies. We want to see the chiefs take over this whole area. It might sound idealistic, but we have technology. I think we can do proper management on our territories, a type of management I think is worthwhile. We're going to make ourselves known. We're going to make sure that people take notice of us from now on. So there's going to be a transition period, but the chiefs want to involve as many people from the local area as we can as well."

It was one of those moments in the meeting when a light seemed to go on in everybody's heads. When the applause had subsided, there were more questions, Marvin George started to speak, and another light clicked on.

There are the Gitksan, he said. They are four clans. The wolf, the frog, the fireweed, the eagle. Then there are the Wet'suwet'en. They also have the wolf, and they have the frog. But they also have the small frog, he said. That's Marvin's clan. Then there's the Wet'suwet'en fireweed, and the beaver. So the Wet'suwet'en have five clans. It's a little different from the Gitksan, but combined, the Gitksan and Wet'suwet'en have 22,000 square miles. Each Gitksan clan is divided into houses. Each house owns a territory of land. The Wet'suwet'en clans have houses too, he said, but they do things a little differently. His clan has three houses. Each house owns a territory of land. In his clan there is the Thin House, the Dark House and the Birchbark House. And it's matrilineal — you belong to your mother's house. But the father's side has privileges on the wife's house side. It might sound complicated at first, but think of it this way, he said: "That's why I don't think I need a permit to go fishing or hunting on my own land ... and that's why we say we own the land. As members of the house, we have responsibilities to the house, to that land. We have responsibilities to look after that land, and see how it is when we pass it on to the next generation. They say 80 years, 120 years to rotate the trees, the crops. How big are they going to be in 120 years? Are they going to be there? You guys should know that. And if they cut down those trees, what's next?"

Then Djogaslee spoke. In his house, he has 300 people to think about, he said. Now there's white people in his country, and he's concerned about them, too.

"I'm concerned about my people and also the non-Indian people who live here. A couple of the young people here earlier, they were saying they were born and raised in this area. This is true ... Macrae over there, I know his dad. And the others, I seen them when they moved into this area. In those days, the way we logged, there were small sawmills, and everybody could work, but it was selective logging. We leave the small trees there so there was no damage. That's what I'd like to see in the area. What's going to happen to our truckers? Our logging contractors? That's why we put up roadblocks right now, to get the government to sit across from us. That's why we called you here tonight, to tell you what our concerns are. We all have children coming up, grandchildren coming up. Let's get together. Not fight one another."

And then came Wii Seeks. There had been questions about who the Indian leaders really were in these houses, what their relationship to the land was exactly, and what it is about the Indians around here that made them that much different from the whites. If there was any real confusion left, Wii Seeks cleared it up for anyone who was listening. Judging by the silence in the hall, everybody was.

"We have always been here, since the beginning of time,"

he began. "We own the land. We are the jurisdiction. For too many years, you and I have all been trained to accept documents from the government, documents from an illegal entity. This question of ownership is only a question in the mind of the government, because it is in their advantage to perceive it as a land question. It is no question to us. We know it belongs to us.

"We are willing to share. We have lived in coexistence for many years. Conditions were not always so easy to endure on our part, but we will not be vindictive. We will continue to sit for hours to find a peaceful resolution. So our generosity has not evaporated. As the task force gets together, the question is, how can you get a share of my forest? How can you acquire permission to fish in my rivers?

"We are an easy people to get along with. We ask you to recognize our jurisdiction and our ownership. You ask, who are your leaders? It is a question my friends ask. Who are your leaders? Well, our leaders are sitting here at this table," he said.

At the front of the hall were Xsimwits'iin, Yagosip, Tenimgyet, Sgenna, Djogaslee, Giila'wa, Niist and the others. "My friends, it is you that is leaderless."

To some extent, for a while at least, things were starting to make sense. As everyone was leaving, people took the time to shake hands, and the white people thanked the women in the kitchen for the fine meal. Spencer told reporters on his way out that the B.C. government had been wrong about the Indian land "question." He said: "We have to get to the table. The government and the natives have to sit down and deal with the issue for some kind of conclusion."

Brian Larson, who'd been shut down by the Suskwa blockade, was still a little bit confused by everything, but he sounded hopeful. "I'm not sure I understand all the issues yet, but as far as the logging's concerned, all you have to do is fly over the Kispiox Valley and see what's been done there in the past ten years."

Sunday night came, and the Kispiox chiefs set up their road-block. This time, it was right out on the pavement, miles from the reserve, within spitting distance of the forest ministry offices. No trucks moved into the Kispiox Monday morning. All hell broke loose. By Mas Gak's reckoning, it would take the chiefs only another six weeks to bring the entire forest industry in the 22,000-square-mile territory to its knees.

The truckers who were turned back by the new roadblock set up a little show of their own on the Yellowhead Highway over at New Town, where they parked about 30 of their rigs and slowed traffic. Forests Minister Dave Parker was on the phone from Victoria to tell New Town mayor Dave Webster that the government would take immediate steps to save his loggers' jobs. Deputy forests minister Ben Marr told reporters the B.C. government was getting an injunction application ready for first thing Tuesday morning. Deputy Attorney-General Ted Hughes was busy clearing his desk for the showdown, which he described as "a very sensitive matter" that was receiving the "undivided attention" of the attorney-general's office.

The message the chiefs delivered to Westar and the logging contractors was plain. Are you really interested in the task force or not? Westar said yes, we're interested. So the new Kispiox blockade lasted about as long as the last one had.

Within two weeks, the B.C. Supreme Court rejected an application by the attorney-general's department for an injunction to prevent the chiefs from any more of that sort of behaviour, the court granted the chiefs' request that Victoria's injunction be adjourned indefinitely, and Judge William Esson also rejected Victoria's request that the chiefs get their

adjournment only if they promised to stop putting up blockades everywhere. Judge Esson also dismissed a similar no-
roadblocks request from a group that had mysteriously
formed somewhere within the labyrinth of the legal system
called the Loggers Defence Alliance. Esson was particularly
annoyed by the nuisance of the loggers' application because
he'd been called back from his lunch to deal with it.

So a new approach it would be, and for now, the roadblocks would stay down, as long as the task force was meeting. The chiefs were willing to wait and see how Westar and
the loggers would behave. Maybe this really was the start of
something, and it was time to give the newcomers a chance.

It was Tuesday, October 31, when Parker called to reassure
Webster that Victoria would stand by New Town in its troubles with the Indians. The same day, Westar and the loggers
told the chiefs, yes, we agree to your task force. It was that
night that Yagosip held onto Sgenna's arm as their pickup
skidded to a stop at the blazing gatehouse. Leave the shotgun
where it is. Next time, it might be different, but for now, let
it alone.

'Noola, the George brothers, Sgenna and Yagosip followed the tire tracks, but they lost him. While they were all
a good distance up the Suskwa Road, whoever it was that
burned the gatehouse had ducked into a sideroad and come
out behind them and headed out of the Suskwa unseen.

Next time, it might be different.

T H E   C O M I N G   F A L L
O F   D I M L A H A M I D

Less than a month had passed since the Suskwa chiefs sat around that table at Gitanmaax hall, when the chiefs studied the map on the table in front of them looking for the best place to move the Suskwa roadblock that had begun deep in the bush. Less than a month had passed since the kitchen camp and the roadblock tents went up on that wooded ridge above the Bulkley River.

About 5,000 years had passed since Skawah returned from the sky and brought her sky-born children to wreak vengeance on the village of Keemalay and establish the great city-state of Dimlahamid on the banks of the 'Ksan, in the shadow of Stegyawden. It had been just about as long since Dizkle was founded, giving rise to the Wet'suwet'en way of understanding the world, with its Dark House, Thin House and Birchbark House, its House of Many Eyes, Sun House and Owl House.

The great city state rose and fell and nobody had been able to find it. Edward Sapir tried, Diamond Jenness tried, Marius

Barbeau tried, Wilson Duff tried. Even B.C. Supreme Court Judge Allan McEachern was willing to give it a try. Then the task would fall to the B.C. Court of Appeal, then maybe the Supreme Court of Canada. By then it could be 1996.

Delgamuukw would be there, but it would not be the Delgamuukw who stood beside Gisday Wa when the chiefs first filed their statement of claim in the Smithers court registry on October 23, 1984. Back then, Delgamuukw was Albert Tait. By the time Delgamuukw arrived in the Smithers courthouse for the opening of the trial in May 1987, Delgamuukw was Kenny Muldoe. When the closing arguments got underway in the same Alfred Avenue courthouse in the spring of 1990, the ascendancy was about to pass again. On April 8, while the lawyers summarized their respective cases, Muldoe was dead, and his body was being carried in a long procession of cars and pickup trucks and four-by-fours back to Kispiox for the beginning of the round of feasts that would conclude with a new Delgamuukw. The chiefs would call Kenny Muldoe by his baby name, and invite their peers to his cremation.

Whatever happened in the court case, the constantly circling whirlpool of Gitksan and Wet'suwet'en names would carry on. Life for some people in the Gitksan and Wet'-suwet'en territories would continue to proceed in the western, linear fashion. But for the Gitksan and Wet'suwet'en, time would also continue to move in cycles. Maybe even long after people had forgotten what the Supreme Court of Canada was, the people in these mountains would know Delgamuukw, Mas Gak, Wii Seeks, 'Noola, Sgenna, Yagosip, Wii Muugalsxw, Haa'txw, and the others.

The task force would come and go. The roadblocks that came down would come up again, and by the final days of July 1990, during the time of a partial eclipse of the sun in B.C.'s vast northwest, there were blockades and highway checkpoints at Gitwangak, Kispiox, and Moricetown. The Manitoba Cree leader Elijah Harper, NDP MLA for Rupertsland, had killed a national constitutional accord, throwing doubt on Quebec's place in Confederation. Armed Mohawk Warrior Society members were staring down armed Quebec police at Oka, Ojibwa and Cree people were blocking highways on the prairies and the CN line was blocked at Gitwangak. Stl'atl'imx people blocked the B.C. Rail line at Shalalth, the Duffey Lake Road and Highway 12 at Pavilion. Haidas had blockaded charter fishing fleets at Duu Guusd. Okanagans had blockaded the Green Mountain Road in their broad valley and Kwagewlths blockaded the Vancouver Island highway at Campbell River. Ottawa's comprehensive claims policy would come and go. B.C.'s refusal to negotiate land claims settlements would one day go, too.

Dimlahamid rises and falls. It was a very real place in linear time, but it was clearly about much more than that.

The first mistake was to use the stomach of a bear as a toy. The first warning was a feather that fell from the sky. The first punishment was the dismemberment of the people of the city. Then they are forgiven, and made whole again.

Again, the people are careless. They abuse the animals, offend the mountain goats. Strange visitors arrive on the outskirts of the city, they lead the people to a feast on Stegyawden, and a massacre ensues. One of the goats spares one of the young goat hunters, and he returns with a new covenant. Dimlahamid is reborn.

The next punishment begins with the rain. It fills the streets of the city, and only those who have remembered the sky people's instructions are saved. Their houses become like ships, and when the waters subside, the people rebuild Dimlahamid.

Then comes the Medeek, the vengeance of the trout spirits who were offended when the women made headdresses from their bones at the Lake of the Summer Pavilions. The

Medeek, like a great bear, arises from the waters of the lake and a terrible war follows. The bear is at last driven off, and it returns to the bottom of the lake.

Then there is the great snowfall, provoked by a diplomatic affront to the nations of salmon. The final dispersal and the last of the great migrations begin when 'Noola, the last chief to leave Dimlahamid, finds Kwiskwas at the edge of the smokehole of his house.

After the final days of October 1989, everybody got down to work on the task force. There were a lot of things to learn, and Keith Spencer and Brian Larson and Dave Webster and Surinder Malhotra couldn't be expected to understand it all at once. Neither could Tom Atrill, with his loyalty to something called Canada, and his allegiance to something else known as British Columbia, and his insistence that the militia be brought in, if necessary, if all this carry-on didn't come to a quick halt.

I remembered the early days of the Suskwa roadblock, after it had been moved out closer to the bridge, when Mas Gak talked about Dimlahamid. People just couldn't sustain such big infrastructures and bureaucracies. But it had been there, with one end somewhere near the Suskwa camp and the other end several miles away somewhere down by Gitsegukla. Maybe two glaciation periods ago. The fact that people hadn't found it was a good thing, he had said. Nobody knew how old it really was, or what it really meant. But it was adjusting to life after Dimlahamid that was interesting, returning to the house territories, becoming part of the spiritual landscape. That's what matters. What it meant for Mas Gak was a lesson, and among many other things, the lesson was that the Gitksan and Wet'suwet'en don't need to tolerate institutions that deny them their rightful power.

He was sitting beside the birchpole tripod at the roadblock

fire, carving a circle in the ground between his boots. The sun was out.

"So that's what's happening," he had said. "That's what it is."

He carved a second circle around the first.

"One of the greatest crimes is the extinction of these great species that have evolved here, like the fish. We try to develop these exotic species, and we do the same thing with forestry. The ministry of forests doesn't have the knowledge or the authority. So we're trying to decentralize things. The whole bureaucracy is going to change. The unions, work, everything. We're seeing that here. We have seasonal type of employment, different professions, multi-professional people. It's a slow decline. Modern states are on the decline.

"Dimlahamid is a physical thing, but it didn't occur just once or twice. The constant thing that goes through it for us is the clan system. That's the ongoing tension throughout our history. So there's a second or a third or a fourth Dimlahamid, happening right now.

"It's happening right now."

THE FALL OF
DIMLAHAMID

Almost a decade after the Suskwa roadblock, Wii Seeks was roaring north in a company pick-up truck on the Kispiox Trail, and the rain was falling from clouds that were slumped against the mountain walls enclosing the ancient house territory of Wii Muugalsxw, the Wolf chief. Wii Seeks was cussing about the grubby old run-down Ford F-150, with its bent frame and its compression gone. The company should have junked it by now, he said. But it rattled along all the same.

Such rain, so soon. Such mud on the road. The Kispiox Trail, the main logging-road artery connecting the cutblocks of the Kispiox Timber Supply Area to pavement and to the mills at South Town and Carnaby and Terrace, should have been hard-packed with snow. But it was getting rutted and soft. It was the same all over the northwest. It was raining on all the logging roads, on the Suskwa and the Salmon, the Kitsegucla and the Cranberry, on Clo Long and Clo Short. It meant breakup was coming early. The snow was starting to melt away from the mountains. It had something to do with El Niño. Everybody was talking about it.

"The end is coming soon," Wii Seeks said. He smiled.

The trial known as *Delgamuukw versus The Queen*, which had begun in Smithers on May 11, 1987, and which reopened in Vancouver the day Adam Gagnon's backhoe blade inadvertently unearthed the shaman's tomb on the hill above Moricetown, had finally gone all the way to the Supreme Court of Canada. Getting there had been an epic journey. The trial before B.C. Supreme Court Justice Allan McEachern had continued off and on for a total of 374 days, until June 30, 1990. More than 70 witnesses gave evidence. There were 9,200 exhibits containing more than 50,000 pages. The plaintiffs alone filed 23 large binders of legal documents. The trial transcript came to more than 26,000 pages, and Judge McEachern still got it wrong.

Describing his own decision as "brutal," McEachern attracted a brief flurry of international attention to himself by suggesting native people were somehow inherently uncivilized because they didn't have wheeled vehicles, by saying that aboriginal life was "nasty, brutish and short," and by saying a lot of other things in defence of his findings, which were largely unprecedented in Canadian law. Among his opinions was that somehow, constitutionally protected aboriginal rights to the land and the land's resources may exist elsewhere in Canada, but not in British Columbia. To provide some sort of balance, McEachern found that the B.C. government was bound to act in a trust-like, non-adversarial manner towards native communities, but beyond that, his decision was a painful dismissal of more than a century of arguments advanced by native leaders and their lawyers. Still, McEachern's ruling had a very brief shelf life. In 1993, the B.C. Court of Appeal overturned McEachern's legal opinions about aboriginal rights, but maintained McEachern's finding that the B.C. government was bound by a fiduciary duty to native peoples. The Appeals Court judges established a new legal regime, one in which the concurrence of Crown sovereignty and aboriginal rights demanded "co-existence" and "reconciliation," and strongly urged negotiated solutions to outstanding grievances. By then, the B.C. government was already beginning to negotiate treaties.

In the dying days of their regime, Social Credit politicians finally came around to the idea of treaties. In 1991, a tripartite body, the B.C. Claims Task Force, composed of Socred and federal Tory appointees and First Nations' representatives, recommended a six-stage treaty process, with a semi-independent treaty commission to oversee the talks. When the New Democratic Party came to power that year, Premier Mike Harcourt pledged to get the B.C. Treaty Commission up and running, although it took almost two years before the commission's doors were finally open. Within months, more than 40 First Nations were making the journey through the six-stage treaty process. While the Nisga'a negotiations were moving close to a treaty (the Nisga'a talks were underway before the B.C. Treaty Commission set up shop), the B.C. Treaty Commission process stumbled along, but it had become mainly an interminable, ongoing shouting match between B.C.'s major resource companies and the NDP government. The NDP progressively narrowed its treaty-making vision throughout the 1990s, and as First Nations' bills mounted (80 per cent of treaty funds to First Nations come in the form of loans), the B.C. government's view of treaties became narrowed further to a cash-and-land formula that would produce treaties consisting of bigger reserves and a one-time cash buyout for native communities. All the while, the Reform Party and the B.C. Liberal Party were making great strides, convincing a weary public that the NDP was "selling the farm" as part of a politically correct agenda of appeasement and liberal guilt, and the best thing would be for treaties to eliminate any separate identity for native people altogether, eliminate "special rights based on race," and ensure "one law for all Canadians." It was all about reviving McEachern's notions, which had been so solidly dismissed by the judge's own peers. Talks with the Gitksan broke down in 1996, so the chiefs went back to court. Then, on December 11, 1997, at the Supreme Court of Canada, the hereditary chiefs were vindicated in all the things they had said to McEachern, and in everything they had said on the Suskwa roadblock, and at every roadblock of every kind since the first one, which was the canoe blockade of the Skeena River in 1872.

What the Supreme Court's six judges said was that aboriginal title was very real, it was protected by the constitution, and it was a form of ownership that no one, certainly not the B.C. government, could continue to pretend wasn't there. It was there in old Canadian law, which did not end at the Rockies, and it was there in songs and in stories told and retold down through the ages. Crown title was there on the land, too, the judges said, and the Crown's authority prevailed; governments could still infringe upon aboriginal title, but it was a delicate business, and it could end up costing money in compensation. In the end, it was all about co-existence, the judges said, and in British Columbia, what remained was the work of reconciliation, and the work of just muddling through. The court also made it plain that people who didn't like these things would be wise to grow up and get over it. Supreme Court Chief Justice Antonio Lamer summed it up this way: "Let us face it. We are all here to stay."

All through the winter, there had been celebration feasts in community halls throughout Gitksan territory. But the way the judges had answered British Columbia's ages-old "Indian land question" was proving terribly upsetting to certain people, particularly all the politicians, newspaper columnists and radio hotline hosts who had championed McEachern's ideas and whose careers had been built by harrumphing about aboriginal rights in a phraseology that had not changed since the colonial era. To them, *Delgamuukw versus The Queen* was a sure sign that the end of the world was indeed upon us all, and that we were all doomed. You couldn't pick up a newspaper or turn on the television without learning more about the looming apocalypse. Wii Seeks found it endlessly amusing.

"Yep," he said. "The end is coming soon."

A voice crackled over the VHF radio, on Kispiox Channel 158.22, "39 loaded." Hard to say who it was. Could have been Roy Simms. Maybe Larry Wookey. But it meant a logging truck was headed south out of the valley, and it had just passed the 39-kilometre board, a bit north of the Murder Main junction.

Another voice. "Where you at, Wii Seeks?" It was Tom Harris, the logging superviser. Wii Seeks picked up the transmitter and answered, "35 empty," which meant he was headed up the valley, at about the 35-kilometre board.

He resumed his line of thought.

"Yep. The end is coming. That's why I changed my ways," he said, straightfaced. "I haven't committed adultery for six months. If Jesus takes me in my sleep, I'm ready."

And then a long silence. And then a burst of laughter, the way Wii Seeks laughs. It goes on and on, and it stops just as suddenly, but there's that smirk there, like it could erupt again at any moment. It was two days away from Wii Seeks' 49th birthday, and in the years since his grandmother's death feast, we'd become great friends. He was now my son Eamonn's godfather, and I was up for a visit. After I left the *Vancouver Sun*, I continued to write, mainly books, but also for magazines. I'd also spent some time working for the B.C. Treaty

Commission, and for a variety of First Nations that were now struggling to make their way through the bureaucratic maze of the treaty process. So I was particularly interested to know what it was that Wii Seeks meant, in conversations going back five years, when he said it wasn't going to matter what the Supreme Court of Canada did. He'd say it didn't matter whether treaties would resolve anything either, because the hereditary chiefs were going ahead and implementing aboriginal title and making peace on their on terms with the non-natives in the territory. It was fine that the highest court in the country had happened to agree with them in these things, but it was like a happy postcript, more than anything else, to a story Wii Seeks said was already unfolding.

And on this particular afternoon, the way the story was unfolding involved Wii Seeks, driving north on the Kispiox Trail in a Carnaby Operations truck with a groaning engine and a Copperside Cafe coffee mug bouncing around the dash. He was heading up to the Kuldo Main, to move a radio frequency board a bit closer to the Kispiox Trail junction because of a near-catastrophe the day before involving two logging trucks that weren't on the same frequency. And it was there on the Kispiox Trail, in the centre of the maelstrom of howling headlines about the dire implications of the Delgamuukw decision, in the heart of the Gitskan territory, that a nice, shiny, red, 1995 F-350 pick-up truck passed us, headed south, at about the 38-kilometre mark.

"There he is," Wii Seeks says. "There goes Delgamuukw."

And indeed it was Delgamuukw, as in *Delgamuukw versus The Queen*, and there was nothing remarkable in the sight. It was just a rather short man, sitting forward, peering over the steering wheel. Delgamuukw was the named plaintiff among the hereditary chiefs who had sued the Crown on behalf of the 50 Gitksan and Wet'suwet'en houses. When the case began, Delgamuukw was Albert Tait. But Albert died, and the name passed to Kenny Muldoe. Then Kenny died, and the name had been passed down to Earl Muldoe, who operates a small logging outfit called Totemland Contracting with his brother George. Totemland Contracting consisted of a couple of skidders, a loader, two excavators, a tractor and a logging truck. Earl Muldoe also happened to be one of the finest carvers and jewelery makers in B.C., but as a carver, he used the name Earl Muldon, with an 'n', because there were so many Muldoes in the local phonebook. Wii Seeks had a sideline marketing his wares. And there he went. Delgamuukw was headed home from work.

Like Wii Seeks, Delgamuukw works on contract with Skeena Cellulose, the troubled, money-losing octopus of a corporation that had emerged from the corporate ruin of Repap Enterprises, a typical merge-and-takeover company that had assumed Westar Timber's holdings throughout the northwest. Repap eventually skipped these mountains leaving $620 million in debts, stripped mountainsides, and an old pulp mill in Prince Rupert that was held together by duct tape and safety pins. Which was just the kind of thing the Office of the Hereditary Chiefs had warned for years would happen. It was a big part of what all those logging road blockades had been about in the first place. And now, Wii Seeks was playing his small part in what the judges had called coexistence and reconciliation, by working for wages, inspecting logging sites, on a job that came out of an agreement negotiated in 1993 between Repap and the houses of Wiigyet, Waigyet and Wii Seeks — an agreement inherited by Skeena Cellulose. The agreement was an effort to ensure that logging practices conformed more closely to the Gitksan view of things. In the deal, Skeena Cellulose affirmed that the three Gitksan houses enjoyed a "right of first refusal" on all logging development in their house territories, but it was a difficult provision to fully implement because it meant skills a lot of Gitksan people didn't have, and money, which was more scarce still. There were provisions governing mutually acceptable logging plans, the protection of cultural, spiritual, medicinal and other values in the house territories, and there were provisions for jointly developed measures to protect fish and wildlife habitat, soil stability and water quality. Wii Seeks said it was a start, at least, and roadblocks could only accomplish so much.

Despite the efforts at the Suskwa and at Sam Green Creek, the Babine River, eventually, had been crossed, and logging was pushing into the virgin bush of the Gitksans' northern territories. It was sad, Wii Seeks said, but the chiefs "couldn't go on forever like that. It was just the same old bunch of us, and there weren't enough of us." Still, there were opportunities now to make logging more a matter of sustainable harvest, and less a matter of mining trees, and oportunities like that were what Wii Seeks' job with Skeena Cellulose was about. His job also meant checking to see that the loggers were following the rules set out under the Forest Practices Code, a relatively enlightened set of standards that had been ushered in by Mike Harcourt's New Democratic Party government. And it meant seeing to it that logging conformed to specific cut-block plans, like the plans set out on Logging Plan Map CP372 Blk. 8, which kept getting tossed at every bump in the road from the seat to the muddy floor by Wii Seeks' feet.

In the end, these were the kinds of things Wii Seeks meant when he talked about how the chiefs were already implementing aboriginal title. The findings of the Supreme Court of Canada in *Delgamuukw versus The Queen* meant a lot of things to a lot of people. Legal scholars, historians, academics, and economists all weighed in during the weeks and months following the decision with a variety of opinions and analyses about what it meant. B.C.'s NDP politicians decided that the appropriate posture was to scratch their heads about it, and hope that the rickety, cumbersome and costly treaty process that kept Indian leaders so busy would remain the Indians' favoured response. B.C.'s Liberal Party — which by the late 1990s included the former Socred politicians and federal Reform party cadre as well — also favoured the treaty process, so long as native people were forced to "cede, surrender and release" all claims of rights and title in exchange for treaties. But in the Gitksan country, with or without treaty, it was sensible and unglamorous work of the kind Wii Seeks was doing on the Kispiox Trail that would follow from Chief Justice Lamer's words about how we were all here to stay. It meant a joint bid by Skeena Cellulose and Delgamuukw's Totemland Contracting for 30,000 cubic meters of timber from the Kispiox Timber Supply Area, which was competing against a bid from another joint venture, between Kispiox Forest Products and the Kispiox Indian Band. It meant business.

It meant Wii Seeks, in the rain, rooting among the two-by-fours in the back of the company pickup, trying to spot that hammer he had thrown back there. He looked under the red jerrycan. He looked under the spare tire. And then he found it, and hammered the "Frequency 158.22 Kispiox" sign to a hastily constructed two-by-four stand. It was too wobbly, so he changed his mind and nailed it instead onto a pole, and scrambled across the snow bank at the side of the Kuldo Main, trying to find the best place for it, where the loggers could see it. Wii Seeks stood on the road and admired his work. It was raining. He was happy.

It was raining all over Gitksan country. It was raining on the non-native towns, on Two Mile and South Town, Old Hazelton and New Hazelton. It was raining on the hemlock forests, and the fir and the pine, and on the Indian towns, on Kispiox and Gitanmaax, on Hagwilget and Glen Vowell, on

Gitsegukla and Gitkwangak, and life went on. Down in Prince Rupert, Gordon Sebastian, the Gitksan lawyer, was losing along with all the other Gitksan old boys in the all-native basketball tournament. The smart money was on Metlakatla or Kincolith. At Wrinch Memorial Hospital in Hazelton, the doctors decided they didn't need to strike along with the other northern doctors. The Wolf clan, with John Field School, was planning for a big gweey'ya, a fund-raising event for the B.C. Children's Hospital in Vancouver. Vicki Russell was finishing up her notes for a presentation at Mountainview United Church on the Gitksan five-year plan. There were bridge club meetings. There was storytime for the toddlers at the library.

At Kispiox School, Wii Muugalsxw the wolf chief, who is also Art Wilson, was standing in a classroom and speaking words in Gitksan, in his quiet voice, to Lloyd Johnson, and then to Vance Shanoss. But the boys were boisterous and demanding. They wanted more crayons. Then they didn't want crayons. They wanted pencils. Wii Muugalsxw was 50 years old, and we laughed when we realized that it was already a decade since we first met on a logging road block-ade he'd had a hand in organizing to try to stop the clearcut-ting of the house territory that Gitksan law had entrusted him to protect. These days, he said, logging practices have never been better. There was a long way to go, but they're better. During the roadblocks, he always said it would be the kids who'd have to live with the Delgamuukw decision, whatever it ended up meaning, and the kids would have to know who they were. Now he is a teacher. He showed me how each of the kids' pictures were different, depending on whether they were frog clan, wolf clan, eagle or fireweed. There are 21 of them in the class, in Grade 2 and Grade 3. A boy named Ben asked if I had a clan. A boy named Kyle asked if I lived in the valley, and a girl named Carlisa told me she was a frog. A little yellow-haired girl named Sarah smiled and showed me what she was colouring. Because she's from a settler family up the valley, she can choose which clan she is. On this day she had chosen to be a wolf.

Far away in Vancouver, the choices the Delgamuukw decision presented could not be so easily made. There was this banner headline in the *Vancouver Sun*: B.C. INDIAN CHIEFS LAY CLAIM TO ENTIRE PROVINCE, RESOURCES. The story reported: "B.C.'s native Indians are laying claim to every tree, every rock, every fish and every animal in the province." It purported to be about the Delgamuukw decision, which B.C.'s native leaders were reported to be "brandishing," but it came as news down at the First Nations Summit, which was the outfit that was reportedly doing the brandishing. They knew nothing at all about the claims the *Sun* said they were laying. B.C. Liberal leader Gordon Campbell, however, had demands of his own, and they were that, because of what Delgamuukw meant, B.C.'s native communities should be forced to surrender the aboriginal title the Supreme Court of Canada had just affirmed. "Cede, surrender and release," Campbell said.

Then there was Melvin H. Smith, a career bureaucrat who did duty as constitutional adviser to the Social Credit government in the days when CKNW chat-show host Rafe Mair was a cabinet minister. After the McEachern decision, Smith's elaborate "land claims" theories had earned him a sort of cult status on B.C.'s hotline circuit. One would have thought that his notoriety would have been as short-lived as the McEachern decision, but as hysteria whipped up by his Reform Party friends took root all over small-town B.C., Smith's star continued to rise, thanks in no small part to Mair's hotline-show forum. Then, in December, 1997, all Smith's theories were tossed finally and unceremoniously into a dumpster behind the Supreme Court buildings in

Ottawa. And so he stood before an assembled gathering of the Vancouver Board of Trade and railed against the Supreme Court judges. He listed all the mistakes they had made in their interpretation of the law. He cited every error in their findings, and castigated them for "one of the most audacious acts of judicial engineering in our history." To Smith, the Delgamuukw decision meant the province was now plunging into "a state of crisis unlike anything it had faced in its 127 years within the Canadian Confederation." Somehow, it was all Mike Harcourt's fault. Governments now had to "abolish" aboriginal title, Smith said. That such a thing would be unconstitutional and unenforceable was a detail Smith said he did "not have time to go into."

Then there was Premier Glen Clark's constitutional adviser, Progressive Democratic Alliance leader and MLA Gordon Wilson (himself a former B.C. Liberal Party leader). Wilson was off to Ottawa to support Quebecers who opposed the federal government's decision to refer the question of Quebec separation to the Supreme Court. To Wilson, the Delgamuukw decision meant the Supreme Court of Canada was telling B.C. how to treat its Indians, and that had to stop. There was Mel Smith's friend and Fraser Institute associate Gordon Gibson, a long-time champion of Smith's eccentric causes (and also a former B.C. Liberal leader), who was writing in the *Globe and Mail* that the Supreme Court judges had made a terrible mistake that would cost taxpayers "several multiples" of $10 billion. Then Smith wrote a letter to the *Globe and Mail* to say how right Gibson was about everything. Then the Fraser Institute's own Owen Lippert was given a full page in the *Vancouver Sun* to castigate Chief Justice Antonio Lamer for being "naive" and for giving "95 per cent of the B.C. land mass to about five per cent of the population." It was all because the judges had allowed themselves to be unduly influenced by "radical utopian law professors."

And then there was Martyn Brown, spokesman for the "Citizens' Voice on Native Claims," which is more or less the same group of resource companies listed as intervenors in the Delgamuukw case, whose arguments had just ended up in the same dumpster with Smith's theories. Brown used to be the Social Credit caucus research director, but he bolted for the Reform Party, and now he was sending off opinion pieces to newspapers saying that the Supreme Court had "flipped our entire land title system on its head." The decision would lead to increased racial tension and would "exacerbate regional alienation," he wrote. It all must have impressed Gordon Campbell, because he promptly hired Brown to serve as the Liberal caucus executive director.

But below the cloud-laden peak of Stegyawden, at the confluence of the Bulkley and the Skeena, no state of crisis was evident. At Two Mile's Hummingbird Cafe, Doug Donaldson, editor of a local newspaper, called *Confluence*, laughed out loud about it all. There were dinosaurs around still, sure, he said. But nobody was afraid of aboriginal title anymore. If there was anything that had been collapsing and frightening people, it was the volume-based, industrial forest economy. The Repap fiasco, which had been inherited by Skeena Cellulose, was now being maintained by the B.C. government, which was pumping tens of millions into the ailing operation and employing the NDP's own brands of duct tape and safety pins: $10,000 payouts to logging contractors for the money they were owed and a dime for every other dollar they had coming over that figure. It was a debacle that shifted the way people tended to think about things, Donaldson said, and it wasn't the hereditary chiefs who were scary anymore. It was the collapse of the forest industry that was scary.

In the streets of Hazelton, at the B.C. Cafe on Omenica Street, at the Shoppers Food Mart around the corner, at the Sunrise Cafe, at the Inlander Hotel and at the Old Salts fish and chip shop, the talk was mainly about winter, which was ending a lot earlier than usual. There was no talk about a crisis into which the Supreme Court had just plunged the province.

"I think all of us are pretty comforted," said Alice Maitland, now 64, and still the well-loved, no-nonsense mayor of Old Town, a job she'd held for 23 years. "As far as I can tell, everybody's pretty happy about the court decision, even the people around here who used to be opposed to land claims." As for Smith, Campbell, Gibson and the rest, Maitland said: "I think the problem there is that they just don't know what they're talking about."

Not that the NDP is much better, she said, with its timidity and its spluttering treaty process, its lack of resolve and its general "messing around." It was just that for Maitland, the Delgamuukw decision meant practical things. Reasonable things. It meant a consortium on economic development issues that the local municipalities were hammering together with the hereditary chiefs. It meant a joint proposal with the hereditary chiefs for a community-based forest licence she was hoping Victoria would approve. It meant a study, undertaken by the Gitksan government, that was looking into why both native and non-native kids in the territory tend to drop out of high school so much. It meant that when the Village of Hazelton wrote a letter complaining about delays in approval for a sewer line, the letter ended up underneath a pile on somebody's desk somewhere, but when the letter went with Gitanmaax Band Council on the letterhead and Delgamuukw's signature on the bottom of it, suddenly, approvals were pending. It was a bit mischievous, Maitland allowed. But what the heck. It worked.

"The Delgamuukw decision is going to allow us up here to do what we all know everybody should have been doing all along," Maitland said. "The decision has brought a lot of contentment here. It means we all have to work together now, which is what we've been trying to do for years. I know it's frightening for people in Vancouver, although it shouldn't be. All I can hope is that one day, the rest of the province will see things the same way we do."

In Telkwa, in the territory of the Gitksans' neighbours, the Wet'suwet'ens — whose chiefs were also plaintiffs in the court case — Herb George met with mayors and business people and community leaders to talk about the Delgamuukw decision and what it meant. It was not as though the doomsaying and fearmongering coming from Vancouver had not affected Telkwa: some people asked George, the Wet'suwet'en hereditary chief who was now the Assembly of First Nations' vice-chief for B.C., whether the Indians were going to take their private property. George said no, and the answer to that question had always been no, and he would keep saying no until he was "blue in the face." What Delgamuukw meant was that the native communities and the settler communities now had something they could build on, for their mutual benefit, George said. It was a good meeting, everyone agreed. Smithers Mayor Brian Northrup said he liked the way things were going, that it could mean a "new era" for the Bulkley Valley, and he would say the same to anyone who wanted to listen.

At the sprawling Carnaby mill downriver from Hazelton, the Skeena Valley opens up a bit and the Seven Sisters mountains hover to the southwest, but there was no sign of the world ending there, either. The forest industry was in turmoil everywhere, but Carnaby's main sawmill was cranking back up, and Paul Veltmeyer, Carnaby's woodlands manager, reckoned that Delgamuukw was probably the least of his worries. All Delgamuukw had meant for him so far was that Wii Seeks had been making some noises about renegotiating things, but Veltmeyer said he reckoned they'd haggle it through all right.

Veltmeyer's introduction to the Gitksan territory took place at a logging road blockade at Kispiox in 1991, with Wii Seeks standing at the head of what Veltmeyer ended up calling Checkpoint Charlie for the rest of that summer. His first conversations with Wii Seeks were about arrangements to allow a silviculture crew past the checkpoint, in and out of the chiefs' traditional territories. And now they were working together, and they could tease each other about those days. Veltmeyer was 23 years old back then. Now, Veltmeyer and his wife, Leslie, a nurse at Wrinch Memorial in Hazelton, live with their six-year-old twins Sean and Millika in a house they just built in New Town. He used nice, tight-grained hemlock for the spindles and risers in the staircase. Not oak. Hemlock. Some of the wood that usually goes into lumber production could produce far greater value, Veltmeyer said. The Gitksans were right when they complained about things like that. Veltmeyer parts company with the Gitksan chiefs a bit when he says the company's doing the best it can with the equipment it's working with. But he said the Gitksan chiefs' plans to team up with local non-native governments on new, community forest tenures in the territory seemed pretty reasonable to him.

"The government has got to get its head around some kind of locally based forestry," Veltmeyer said. "But the leadership here has really got to push it to the next level, like secondary manufacturing, which doesn't really exist here yet. Some of those Gitksan guys, they're brilliant guys. If they could get their heads around those things, we'd all be better off. If we could put our collective brainpower together here, things could really come off the ground."

If there was anywhere at all in Gitksan country where

anyone was planning to plunge British Columbia into what Melvin H. Smith called a state of crisis unlike anything it had faced in its 127 years within the Canadian Confederation, it would have been at Mas Gak's house. For close to twenty years, Mas Gak had been the chief strategist in the Gitksans' struggle to re-establish their traditional authority out on the land. He was also the Gitksans' chief negotiator in the treaty talks. But from his home high above Gitanmaax, perched on a ridge above Two Mile, there was just Mas Gak, also known as Don Ryan, with his wife Sheila, who was now the principal of Hazelton Amalgamated High school, and they were getting ready to sit down to dinner. Mas Gak had cooked spaghetti for Wii Seeks' birthday, and we toasted Wii Seeks with a glass of dry white wine and joked about how all of us were getting older, sometimes a bit faster than we might have liked.

For Mas Gak, there was no magic bullet in the Delgamuukw decision. There were only new opportunities and challenges. He had sent Premier Glen Clark a letter containing a "draft reconciliation agreement" between B.C. and the hereditary chiefs. The agreement set out proposed areas of discussion, such as co-management, consultation standards and forest tenure reform, but Clark's office replied with only a nervous "we'll get back to you" response. It was at least consistent with the bureaucratic head-scratching process the government had embarked upon in order to come to terms with the Delgamuukw decision.

There was no point in holding one's breath, Mas Gak said. The Gitksan had already been waiting four years for movement from Ottawa on a self-government agreement that federal negotiators had initialled. It was a way to get out from under the Indian Act, and to break free from the reserve system. He was not holding his breath waiting for Ottawa to put that agreement in place either.

It was not like there was a great rush. After Delgamuukw, it would take time for things to sink in, he said, and the hereditary chiefs had to weigh things, too. One option was to go back to square one. That was possible. The Supreme Court of Canada ruled that Judge McEachern had made so many "worrisome" errors during the trial that "the factual findings cannot stand," as Chief Justice Lamer put it, and offered the Gitksan the opportunity of a new trial.

Another option was to wait and see whether Canada, B.C. and the First Nations Summit could come up with a treaty process that made room for something other than the cash-and-land model the governments wanted. It was a model the Gitksan and Wet'suwet'en had always opposed, but the B.C. government's unwillingness to abandon it was what caused the Gitksan treaty talks to collapse in 1996. If the governments were willing to discuss something more in line with co-existence and co-management, then maybe treaty talks could resume, Mas Gak said.

Or maybe it would be best just to scrap the treaty process, and turn the B.C. Treaty Commission into some kind of "commission of reconciliation." Maybe the B.C. Supreme Court could appoint some kind of judges' panel to oversee things as they developed. Maybe a lot of things.

"Whatever happens, we have a lot of space now," he said. "We have some real political space."

If the governments tried to over-ride the law or took measures to somehow get out from under it, then who knows, he said. It could be a dogfight. Maybe the roadblocks would come back up again. Everywhere.

Wii Seeks perked up a bit.

"Roadblocks aren't so bad," he said. And he laughed, with that smirk of his lingering. And then Mas Gak laughed.

It was Wii Seeks' birthday. He was happy.

Whatever happened, the hereditary chiefs would continue

to assert aboriginal title, Mas Gak said. It was all about making room for people to get out of the despair of the reserves, become self-reliant again, and reclaim their rightful place back in their house territories. That was the objective, he said, and the chiefs would continue, as best they could, to do those things in cooperation with the local non-native communities.

"That's the objective," Wii Seeks agreed. "We haven't even started yet. It's not just us that's been screwed by the government. It's the white people around here, too. We're always at everybody else's mercy, like a bunch of baby birds with their beaks open, waiting to be fed. That's going to be the way until we start managing our own resources around here, and I think the decision will help."

The Delgamuukw decision also meant that when it came to understanding the land itself, governments were now obliged to listen when old people talked about the adventures of Wiigyet, the giant who is sometimes raven, and about the wars waged by Medeek, the great bear, and about ancient feasts among the mountain goat people of Stegyawden. In our courts, these old stories now carried equal evidentiary weight with Hudson's Bay Company records, mineral-deposit assessments, and timber supply analyses, and these different types of intelligence had to be reconciled. It was the law. It was like we had all finally arrived, somehow, as a country, in this simple thing.

On the land, events had unfolded in the years since the Suskwa in a way much as Mas Gak had anticipated. All those years ago, sitting at the birchpole tripod beside the fire at the Suskwa roadblock, Mas Gak had said that whatever happened in the court case, the Gitksan and the Wet'suwet'en would soldier on. There would be no happily ever after. The provincial government's longstanding refusal to negotiate treaties would collapse, he'd said back then, and collapse it did. The task force set up after the Gitksan logging road blockades would come and go, he'd said back then. It came and went. Westar would collapse in the northwest, he'd said. Westar collapsed. Dimlahamid rises and falls. He'd talked then about the great crime of extinction which was being committed then, particularly against salmon populations throughout the Skeena watershed. In the years since the Suskwa roadblock, the entire north coast salmon fishing industry had come close to collapse, partly because of plain old overfishing, partly because of price collapses, partly because of the forest industry's prolonged thrashing of habitat, and partly because of conservation closures to protect small stocks that had been perilously weakened by indiscriminate "mixed-stock" fishing in the gillnet fisheries at the mouth of the Skeena. In the late 1980s, for instance, the Upper Morice coho salmon were still spawning in the thousands, but by 1998, a dozen Upper Morice coho reached the spawning grounds.

And while conferences, public debates and government workshops proceeded across B.C. in Delgamuukw's wake, the one question that remained was whether British Columbia was yet mature enough to participate in the conclusion of honorable treaties with First Nations. The law, such as it is, has almost always been on the "Indian side" in Canada. This has been true since a century before Confederation, since the Royal Proclamation of 1763. It is what politicians do with the law that matters, and what the public instructs politicians to do is what ultimately counts.

Still, the Delgamuukw decision was something to be hopeful about, Mas Gak conceded. It bought some time. Nothing had changed in the long-term plans Mas Gak had articulated all those years ago. Back then, Mas Gak was talking about co-existence and reconciliation, and in the end, there was nothing necessarily romantic or glamorous about these things. For Wii Seeks, they meant getting up early the next morning to head up the Kuldo Main to do some safety checks, and to make sure the skidders weren't getting too close to the machine-free zones around the creeks. That kind of thing. It was about muddling through, with "good faith, and give and take on all sides," as Judge Lamer had put it.

It meant facing the fact that when all was said and done, we are all here to stay.

*The author with Wii Seeks, somewhere in the Babine country
near the old village of Kisgegas, 1989.*

EXCERPTS FROM

DELGAMUUKW

VERSUS THE QUEEN

Excerpts from Chief Justice Lamer's written reasons, Delgamuukw
versus The Queen, *December 11, 1997:*

Aboriginal title encompasses the right to exclusive use and occupation of the land held pursuant to that title for a variety of purposes, which need not be aspects of those aboriginal practices,
customs and traditions which are integral to distinctive aboriginal cultures. The protected uses must not be irreconcilable with
the nature of the group's attachment to that land.

Aboriginal title is *sui generis,* and so distinguished from other
proprietary interests, and characterized by several dimensions. It
is inalienable and cannot be transferred, sold or surrendered to
anyone other than the Crown. Another dimension of aboriginal
title is its sources: its recognition by the Royal Proclamation,
1763 and the relationship between the common law which rec-
ognizes occupation as proof of possession and systems of aboriginal law pre-existing assertion of British sovereignty. Finally, aboriginal title is held communally.

The exclusive right to use the land is not restricted to the right to engage in activities which are aspects of aboriginal practices, customs and traditions integral to the claimant group's distinctive aboriginal culture. Canadian jurisprudence on aboriginal title frames the "right to occupy and possess" in broad terms and, significantly, is not qualified by the restriction that use be tied to practice, custom or tradition. The nature of the Indian interest in reserve land which has been found to be the same as the interest in tribal lands is very broad and incorporates present-day needs. Finally, aboriginal title encompasses mineral rights and lands held pursuant to aboriginal title should be capable of exploitation. Such a use is certainly not a traditional one.

The content of aboriginal title contains an inherent limit in that lands so held cannot be used in a manner that is irreconcilable with the nature of the claimants' attachment to those lands. This inherent limit arises because the relationship of an aboriginal community with its land should not be prevented from continuing into the future. Occupancy is determined by reference to the activities that have taken place on the land and the uses to which the land has been put by the particular group. If lands are so occupied, there will exist a special bond between the group and the land in question such that the land will be part of the definition of the group's distinctive culture. Land held by virtue of aboriginal title may not be alienated because the land has an inherent and unique value in itself, which is enjoyed by the community with aboriginal title to it. The community cannot put the land to uses which would destroy that value. Finally, the importance of the continuity of the relationship between an aboriginal community and its land, and the non-economic or inherent value of that land, should not be taken to detract from the possibility of surrender to the Crown in exchange for valuable consideration. On the contrary, the idea of surrender reinforces the conclusion that aboriginal title is limited. If aboriginal peoples wish to use their lands in a way that aboriginal title does not permit, then they must surrender those lands and convert them into non-title lands to do so.

Aboriginal title at common law was recognized well before 1982 and is accordingly protected in its full form by s. 35(1). The constitutionalization of common law aboriginal rights, however, does not mean that those rights exhaust the content of s. 35(1). The existence of an aboriginal right at common law is sufficient, but not necessary, for the recognition and affirmation of that right by s. 35(1).

Constitutionally recognized aboriginal rights fall along a spectrum with respect to their degree of connection with the land. At the one end are those aboriginal rights which are practices, customs and traditions integral to the distinctive aboriginal culture of the group claiming the right but where the use and occupation of the land where the activity is taking place is not sufficient to support a claim of title to the land. In the middle are activities which, out of necessity, take place on land and indeed, might be intimately related to a particular piece of land. Although an aboriginal group may not be able to demonstrate title to the land, it may nevertheless have a site-specific right to engage in a particular activity. At the other end of the spectrum is aboriginal title itself which confers more than the right to engage in site-specific activities which are aspects of the practices, customs and traditions of distinctive aboriginal cultures. Site-specific rights can be made out even if title cannot. Because aboriginal rights can vary with respect to their degree of connection with the land, some aboriginal groups may be unable to make out a claim to title, but will nevertheless possess aboriginal rights that are recognized and affirmed by s. 35(1), including site-specific rights to engage in particular activities.

Aboriginal title is a right to the land itself. That land may be used, subject to the inherent limitations of aboriginal title, for a variety of activities, none of which need be individually protected as aboriginal rights under s. 35(1). Those activities are parasitic on the underlying title. Section 35(1), since its purpose is to reconcile the prior presence of aboriginal peoples with the assertion of Crown sovereignty, must recognize and affirm both aspects of that prior presence — first, the occupation of land, and second, the prior social organization and distinctive cultures of aboriginal peoples on that land.

The test for the identification of aboriginal rights to engage in particular activities and the test for the identification of aboriginal title, although broadly similar, are distinct in two ways. First, under the test for aboriginal title, the requirement that the land be integral to the distinctive culture of the claimants is subsumed by the requirement of occupancy. Second, whereas the time for the identification of aboriginal rights is the time of first contact, the time for the identification of aboriginal title is the time at which the Crown asserted sovereignty over the land.

In order to establish a claim to aboriginal title, the aboriginal group asserting the claim must establish that it occupied the lands in question at the time at which the Crown asserted sovereignty over the land subject to the title. In the context of aboriginal title, sovereignty is the appropriate time period to consider for several reasons. First, from a theoretical standpoint, aboriginal title arises out of prior occupation of the land by aboriginal peoples and out of the relationship between the common law and pre-existing systems of aboriginal law. Aboriginal title is a burden on the Crown's underlying title. The Crown, however, did not gain this title until it asserted sovereignty and it makes no sense to speak of a burden on the underlying title before that title existed. Aboriginal title crystallized at the time sovereignty was asserted. Second, aboriginal title does not raise the problem of distinguishing between distinctive, integral aboriginal practices, customs and traditions and those influenced or introduced by European contact. Under common law, the act of occupation or possession is sufficient to ground aboriginal title and it is not necessary to prove that the land was a distinctive or integral part of the aboriginal society before the arrival of Europeans. Finally, the date of sovereignty is more certain than the date of first contact.

Both the common law and the aboriginal perspective on land should be taken into account in establishing the proof of occupancy. At common law, the fact of physical occupation is proof of possession at law, which in turn will ground title to the land. Physical occupation may be established in a variety of ways, ranging from the construction of dwellings through cultivation and enclosure of fields to regular use of definite tracts of land for hunting, fishing or otherwise exploiting its resources. In considering whether occupation sufficient to ground title is established, the group's size, manner of life, material resources, and technological abilities, and the character of the lands claimed must be taken into account. Given the occupancy requirement, it was not necessary to include as part of the test for aboriginal title whether a group demonstrated a connection with the piece of land as being of central significance to its distinctive culture.

Ultimately, the question of physical occupation is one of fact to be determined at trial.

If present occupation is relied on as proof of occupation pre-sovereignty, there must be a continuity between present and pre-sovereignty occupation. Since conclusive evidence of pre-sovereignty occupation may be difficult, an aboriginal community may provide evidence of present occupation as proof of pre-sovereignty occupation in support of a claim to aboriginal title. An unbroken chain of continuity need not be established between present and prior occupation. The fact that the nature of occupation has changed would not ordinarily preclude a claim for aboriginal title, as long as a substantial connection between the people and the land is maintained. The only limitation on this principle might be that the land not be used in ways which are inconsistent with continued use by future generations of aboriginals.

At sovereignty, occupation must have been exclusive. This requirement flows from the definition of aboriginal title itself, which is defined in terms of the right to exclusive use and occupation of land. The test must take into account the context of the aboriginal society at the time of sovereignty. The requirement of exclusive occupancy and the possibility of joint title can be reconciled by recognizing that joint title can arise from shared exclusivity. As well, shared, non-exclusive aboriginal rights short of aboriginal title but tied to the land and permitting a number of uses can be established if exclusivity cannot be proved. The common law should develop to recognize aboriginal rights as they were recognized by either *de facto* practice or by aboriginal systems of governance.

Infringement

Constitutionally recognized aboriginal rights are not absolute and may be infringed by the federal and provincial governments if the infringement (1) furthers a compelling and substantial legislative objective and (2) is consistent with the special fiduciary relationship between the Crown and the aboriginal peoples. The development of agriculture, forestry, mining and hydroelectric power, the general economic development of the interior of British Columbia, protection of the environment or endangered species, and the building of infrastructure and the settlement of foreign populations to support those aims, are objectives consistent with this purpose. Three aspects of aboriginal title are relevant to the second part of the test. First, the right to exclusive use and occupation of land is relevant to the degree of scrutiny of the infringing measure or action. Second, the right to choose to what uses land can be put, subject to the ultimate limit that those uses cannot destroy the ability of the land to sustain future generations of aboriginal peoples, suggests that the fiduciary relationship between the Crown and aboriginal peoples may be satisfied by the involvement of aboriginal peoples in decisions taken with respect to their lands. There is always a duty of consultation and, in most cases, the duty will be significantly deeper than mere consultation. And third, lands held pursuant to aboriginal title have an inescapable economic component which suggests that compensation is relevant to the question of justification as well. Fair compensation will ordinarily be required when aboriginal title is infringed....

From Lamer's conclusions:

Finally, this litigation has been both long and expensive, not only in economic but in human terms as well. By ordering a new trial, I do not necessarily encourage the parties to proceed to litigation and to settle their dispute through the courts. As was said in Sparrow, at p. 1105, s. 35(1) "provides a solid constitutional base upon which subsequent negotiations can take place". Those negotiations should also include other aboriginal nations which have a stake in the territory claimed. Moreover, the Crown is under a moral, if not a legal, duty to enter into and conduct those negotiations in good faith. Ultimately, it is through negotiated settlements, with good faith and give and take on all sides, reinforced by the judgments of this Court, that we will achieve what I stated in Van der Peet, *supra,* at para. 31, to be a basic purpose of s. 35(1) — "the reconciliation of the pre-existence of aboriginal societies with the sovereignty of the Crown". Let us face it, we are all here to stay.

BIBLIOGRAPHY

Abbott, Donald, ed. *The World is as Sharp as a Knife: An Anthology in Honour of Wilson Duff*. Victoria: British Columbia Provincial Museum, 1981.

Akrigg, G. P. V., and Helen B. Akrigg. *British Columbia Chronicle*. 2 vols. Vancouver: Discovery Press, 1977.

Attorney-General of B.C. v. Lawrence Wale et al. "Reasons for Judgment," Justice McLachlin, B.C. Court of Appeal, December 17, 1986.

Barbeau, Marius. *The Downfall of Temlaham*. 1928; reprint: Edmonton: Hurtig Publishers, 1973.

—— *Totem Poles of the Gitksan*. Ottawa: National Museum of Canada, 1929.

Berger, Thomas R. "Native History, Native Claims and Self-Determination." *B.C. Studies*, 57, Spring 1983.

Borden, Charles E. "Results of Archeological Investigations in Central British Columbia." *Anthropology in British Columbia*, 3, 1952.

British Columbia. *Papers Relating to the Indian Land Question,*

1850-1875. Victoria: Queen's Printer, 1876.

Cail, Robert E. Land, *Man and the Law: The Disposal of Crown Lands in British Columbia, 1871-1913*. Vancouver: University of British Columbia Press, 1974.

Canada. Department of Indian Affairs. Various communications, Indian agents' reports, trial transcripts, etc., relating to the enforcement of the "potlatch" and "tamanawas" laws, 1913-1924. Photocopies in author's possession.

Canada. Department of Indian and Northern Affairs. *Basic Departmental Data*. Ottawa: The Queen's Printer, 1989.

Cassidy, Frank, and Norman Dale. *After Native Claims? The Implications of Comprehensive Claims Settlements for Natural Resources in British Columbia*. Lantzville, B.C.: Oolichan Books, 1988.

Coupland, Gary. "Evolution of the Lower Skeena Cultural System." Paper presented to the Circum-Pacific Prehistory Conference, Seattle, Wa., August 1-6, 1989.

Davis, Nancy Yaw. "The Zuni-Japanese Enigma." Paper presented to the Circum-Pacific Prehistory Conference, Seattle, Wa., August 1-6, 1989.

Delgamuukw v. The Queen. Supreme Court of Canada, December 11, 1997

Delgamuukw v. The Queen. "Statement of Defence, Her Majesty the Queen in Right of the Province of British Columbia, further amended," September 25, 1986. "Statement of Defence, Her Majesty the Queen in Right of the Province of British Columbia, further amended," Supreme Court of British Columbia, September 25, 1986.

—— "Opening Statement of the Gitksan and Wet'suwet'en Hereditary Chiefs to Chief Justice McEachern of the Supreme Court of B.C.," Supreme Court of British Columbia, May 11, 1987.

—— *Our Box Was Full. Opinion Evidence on the Gitksan and Wet'suwet'en Economy*, Richard Daly. Supreme Court of British

Columbia, March, 1988.

Drake-Terry, Joanne. *The Same as Yesterday: The Lillooet Chronicle the Theft of Their Lands and Resources*. Lillooet, B.C.: Lillooet Tribal Council, 1989.

Drucker, Philip. *Cultures of the North Pacific Coast*. New York: Chandler Publishing, 1965.

—— *Indians of the Northwest Coast*. Garden City, N.Y.: American Museum Science Books, 1955.

Duff, Wilson. *The Indian History of British Columbia*. Vol. 1. Victoria: Provincial Museum of British Columbia, 1964.

Fagan, Brian M. *The Great Journey: The Peopling of Ancient America*. London: Thames and Hudson, 1987.

Fang Zhongpu. "Did Chinese Buddhists Reach America 1,000 Years Before Columbus?" *China Reconstructs*, 29:8, August 1980.

Fisher, Robin. *Contact and Conflict: Indian-European Relations in British Columbia, 1774-1890*. Vancouver: University of British Columbia Press, 1977.

Fladmark, Knut R. *British Columbia Prehistory*. Ottawa: National Museum of Man, 1986.

Gibbs, Richard. "Racism, Hypocrisy and Dishonesty: A Brief Survey of the Indian Land Question in British Columbia." Unpublished paper. Prince George, 1988.

Gitksan-Wet'suwet'en Hereditary Chiefs, library, Hazelton. "The Origin of Gitra'ata." Clifton Heber, Hartley Bay; translated by William Beynon. Unpublished document, 1952.

—— "Migration Down the Skeena River." Clifton Heber, Hartley Bay; recorded by William Beynon. Unpublished document, 1948.

—— "Comments on the Smogelgem Succession." Johnny David, Moricetown. Unpublished document, October 11, 1985.

—— "Patterns of Tension." In *History of the Gitksan and Wet'suwet'en, 1850-*, by Robert Galois. Unpublished, n.d.

—— "The Larhsai'l of Kunradal." Isaac Tens, Gitanmaax, translated by William Beynon. Unpublished document, 1942.

—— Various transcripts, chiefs and elders' interviews, notes on migrations and origins, anthropologists' field notes and ada'ox summaries.

Glavin, Anthony. "Native Claims, Native Rights, and Government Policy: An Historic Account of the Land Claims Issue in British Columbia." Unpublished paper. Simon Fraser University, 1988.

—— "Aboriginal Peoples and Canadian Constitutional Reform, 1978-1988." Unpublished paper. University of British Columbia, 1989.

—— "B.C. Government Policy and Aboriginal Title: An Analysis of the 'Post-Calder' Era." Unpublished paper. University of British Columbia, 1989.

Glavin, Terry. Miscellaneous articles. *Vancouver Sun*, 1986-89.

Haig-Brown, Celia. *Resistance and Renewal: Surviving the Indian Residential School.* Vancouver: Tillacum Library, 1988.

Harris, Kenneth B. (Hagbegwatku), with Frances P. Robinson. *Visitors Who Never Left.* Vancouver: University of British Columbia Press, 1974.

Howay, F. W. *British Columbia: From the Earliest Times to the Present.* Vol. 2. Vancouver: S. J. Clarke, 1914.

Hume, Mark. Miscellaneous articles. *Vancouver Sun*, 1986-89.

Jenness, Diamond. "The Carrier Indians of the Bulkley Valley: Their Social and Religious Life." Smithsonian Institute, Bureau of American Ethnology, *Bulletin* 133, 1943.

Jolles, Carol Zane. "Late 19th and Early 20th Century Euro-American Contact and its Effects on the Yupik Population of St. Lawrence Island: An Ethnohistorical Reconstruction." Paper presented to the Circum-Pacific Prehistory Conference, Seattle, Wa., August 1-6, 1989.

Keddie, Grant. "The Question of Asiatic Objects on the North Pacific Coast of America: Historic or Prehistoric?" Royal British Columbia Museum, *Contributions to Human History*, 3, n.d.

—— "The Reliability of Dating Archeological and Ethnographical Materials with Associated Chinese Coins." Royal British Columbia Museum, Heritage Conservation Branch, *Datum*, 3:2, 1978.

—— "Symbolism and Context: The World History of the Labret and Cultural Diffusion on the Pacific Rim." Paper presented to the Circum-Pacific Prehistory Conference, Seattle, Wa., August 1-6, 1989.

Kendrick, John. *The Men With Wooden Feet: The Spanish Exploration of the Pacific Northwest.* Toronto: NC Press, 1985.

Kahki, Aziz, and Kam Prasad. *Depiction and Perception: Native Indians and Visible Minorities in the Media.* Vancouver: Ad Hoc Committee on Race Relations, 1988.

Knight, Rolf. *Indians at Work: An Informal History of Native Indian Labour in British Columbia, 1858-1930.* Revised edition, Vancouver: New Star Books, 1996.

Krasheninnikov, S. P. *The History of the Kamtschatka and Kurilski Islands, with the Countries Adjacent.* St. Petersburg: 1754; reprint, Chicago: Quadrangle Books, 1962.

LaViolette, Forrest E. *The Struggle For Survival: Indian Cultures and the Protestant Ethic in British Columbia.* Toronto: University of Toronto Press, 1961.

Lillard, Charles, ed. *The Ghostland People: A Documentary History of the Queen Charlotte Islands, 1859-1906.* Victoria: Sono Nis, 1989.

"Log Exports." A Presentation to the Standing Committee on Forests and Lands, British Columbia Legislative Assembly, by Westar Timber Ltd., September 19, 1989.

Manthorpe, Jonathan. "Canadians confused on natives, study says." *Vancouver Sun*, February 11, 1989, p. B2.

Bibliography

Mathias, Chief Joe. "Conspiracy of Legislation." Unpublished. Squamish, January 21, 1986.

Maud, Ralph. *A Guide to B.C. Indian Myth and Legend.* Vancouver: Talonbooks, 1982.

McMillan, Alan D. *Native Peoples and Cultures of Canada.* Vancouver: Douglas and McIntyre, 1988.

Parfitt, Ben. Miscellaneous articles. *Vancouver Sun,* 1986-89.

Raunet, Daniel. *Without Surrender, Without Consent.* Vancouver: Douglas and McIntyre, 1984.

Rosman, Abraham, and Paula Rubel. *Feasting With Mine Enemy.* New York: Columbia University Press, 1971.

Royal Commission on Indian Affairs for the Province of British Columbia (McKenna-McBride Commission). *Report.* Victoria: Queen's Printer, 1915.

Scholefield, E. O. S. *British Columbia: From the Earliest Times to the Present.* Vol. 1. Vancouver: S. J. Clarke, 1914.

Sewid-Smith, Daisy. *Prosecution or Persecution.* Alert Bay, B.C.: Nu-Yum-Baleess Society, 1979.

Stenger, Allison. "Japanese Influenced Ceramics in Pre-Contact Washington State: A View of the Wares and their Possible Origins." Paper presented to the Circum-Pacific Prehistory Conference, Seattle, Wa., August 1-6, 1989.

Titley, E. Brian. *A Narrow Vision: Duncan Campbell Scott and the Administration of Indian Affairs in Canada.* Vancouver: University of British Columbia Press, 1986.

Veillette, John, and Gary White. *Early Indian Village Churches.* Vancouver: University of British Columbia Press, 1977.

Weatherford, Jack. *Indian Givers: How Indians of the Americas Transformed the World.* Crown Publishers, 1988.

Westar Timber v. Don Ryan et al., and *Formula Contractors v. Herb George* et al. "Reasons for Judgment," Justices Carrothers, Esson and Locke, B.C. Court of Appeal, June 9, 1989.

—— "Reasons for Judgment," Justice MacDonell, Supreme Court of B.C., October 21, 1988.

—— "Affidavit." Pete Weeber. Supreme Court of B.C., Hazelton, September 30, 1988.